A Guide to Exhibit Animals

in the
John G. Shedd Aquarium

How to Use This Book

To find information about an exhibit animal or its representative group, use the **Index,** pages 258 to 270, and the names on the overhead signs.

   Not all the animals described will be on exhibit at any one time, nor will all the species exhibited always be found in this guide.

Unicornfish
Naso unicornus

ISBN:0-9611074-0-5

Shedd Aquarium Society, Chicago, Illinois

Cover:
Harlequin tusk fish
Lienardella fasciata

Page one:
Ocellated dragonet
Synchiropus picturatus

Printed in the United States of America.

Contents

Welcome

Welcome to the John G. Shedd Aquarium, located in Grant Park on the shore of Lake Michigan... a place to develop an understanding of man's relationship to the aquatic environment.

The oceans, rivers and lakes covering our planet teem with life. This great group of animals taxes the imagination with a diversity of form, color, habit and size displayed by many species. A sampling of these, over 5,000 fishes, plus invertebrates, reptiles, amphibians, birds and mammals, lives in the Aquarium.

No two visits are ever likely to be the same. The Aquarium's population of aquatic creatures is constantly changing and, as new and different species are acquired, exhibits are created to highlight their particular adaptations.

For over fifty years, the tradition of "accommodating everything in marine life from the most minute fresh- and saltwater denizens to wonders from far-off seas" has been carried on by the Aquarium staff with the support and direction of the Shedd Aquarium Society.

The continuing popularity of the Aquarium is indicated by the more than one million persons that visit annually. Through its many exhibits and fine educational programs, it has become known as "The Ocean by the Lake."

As you travel through the Aquarium, consider the words of naturalist Loren Eiseley: "If there is magic on this planet, it is contained in water."

—William P. Braker, Director

History
The First Fifty Years

John Graves Shedd   1850-1926

John G. Shedd

The world's largest indoor aquarium was a gift to the people of Chicago
from John Graves Shedd, president and chairman of the board of Marshall
Field and Company.

"John Graves Shedd was born on July 20, 1850, on a rocky New Hampshire
farm where he remained until he was seventeen years old. These years spent
under the rigorous conditions of life on a New England farm played an
important part in forming the character of the future merchant. Here he early
learned the value of hard work and thrift and fostered the ambition that
eventually carried him to the top of his chosen field.

After leaving the farm, he worked as a clerk in various stores in nearby
towns until 1872, when he came to Chicago and became associated with
Marshall Field. His rise was steady and rapid until, at the death of Mr. Field
in 1906, he became president of Marshall Field & Company. He held this
position for seventeen years, retiring in 1923 to become chairman of the board
of the same company, a position which he held until his death on October 22,
1926.

Despite the great demands of the management of a great mercantile
establishment, Mr. Shedd found time and energy to devote to many civic and
philanthropic activities. He was actively connected with the Chicago
Planning Commission and was a director and benefactor of various
charitable enterprises.

Shortly before his death he presented $3,000,000 to the people of Chicago
with which to build an aquarium. His choice was influenced by the belief that
an aquarium would provide instructive entertainment for a larger number of
individuals than any other type of institution. The attendance at the splendid
aquarium that now bears his name has proved that he was right. He
entrusted the management of the project to a group of representative
business men organized as the Shedd Aquarium Society. Mr. Shedd passed
away before the project was accomplished but the Society carried on the work
and the completed John G. Shedd Aquarium is as near as possible to what its
founder wished it to be.

The Board of Trustees was originally composed of men who were
associated with Mr. Shedd in various activities. Intimately familiar with his
long and useful life as a great merchant, civic leader, philanthropist,
husband, father and friend, they deemed it a privilege to be chosen to direct
the destinies of this fine institution. They acknowledged the responsibility
placed on them and pledged themselves to so administer the trust that the
John G. Shedd Aquarium would continue to be a fitting memorial to its donor
and a lasting credit to the city he loved."

Melvin A. Traylor
President, Shedd Aquarium Society
1924 - 1934

—from *Guide to the John G. Shedd Aquarium*, 1933.

The Aquarium

*More information about the public displays may be found in **Exhibits**, p 14.*

*Particulars about specific tank sizes, water capacity, etc., is contained in **Behind the Scenes**, p 252.*

Although John G. Shedd did not live to see the Aquarium completed, his family and the recently formed Shedd Aquarium Society carried on his plans to build one larger than any in existence.

From 1924 to 1927, the foremost aquariums around the world were visited, and their best features incorporated into the plans. Many of these remain unparalleled today: the number of exhibits, extensive skylights, vast reservoirs and spacious work areas.

The Chicago architectural firm of Graham, Anderson, Probst and White designed the Aquarium in classic Greek style to harmonize with the neighboring Field Museum of Natural History.

Ground was broken on November 2, 1927, on Park District property next to Lake Michigan. It took two years and $3.25 million to complete the 300-foot diameter, octagonal building of white Georgia marble.

The bronze doors opened to the public for the first time in December, 1929, although the exhibit halls were not yet stocked with fish. Only the swamp was completed, a 40-foot wide sunken pool in the skylit rotunda, filled with semi-tropical plants, reptiles and fish. Forty years later, the pool would be replaced by the first major new display — a sophisticated reproduction of a Caribbean coral reef.

The first of the six galleries opened to a crowd of 20,000 on May 30, 1930. When the Balanced Aquarium Room, later renamed Tributaries, finally opened in June, 1931, the Aquarium housed the greatest variety of sea life under one roof. Public response was overwhelming; more than four million visitors were recorded during that first full year of operation.

The Aquarium's "wonders from far-off seas" were originally identified for visitors by hand-painted glass signs that related to the 1933 guidebook, reprinted until 1968. It was during the late 1960s that a major renovation effort began, resulting in a new information system, more comfortable galleries, improved displays and life support equipment and many expanded programs for the public.

The building itself has changed little. Public exhibits fill only one-third of it, the main floor, while the mezzanine and basement are occupied by offices, the Aquatic Science Center and a vast network of pumps, filters, reservoirs and 75 miles of pipe.

To keep saltwater fishes over 1,000 miles from the nearest ocean coast, the Aquarium had to bring its first million gallons of salt water from Key West, Florida, in 160 railroad tank cars at a cost of about $50,000 or 4 cents a gallon, in 1930.

Splendid aquatic motifs are found in the marble and tile throughout the interior and exterior of the building. The marble in the foyer was set so as to create the effect of waves.

On entering the front doors with their wealth of beautifully molded bronze designs, the visitor steps into the spacious foyer.

Through lofty arches, the six dark exhibit galleries radiate from the central rotunda that houses the 90,000-gallon Coral Reef Exhibit. Tributaries, a separate exhibit area, is located on the left. To the right, beyond the information station, is the auditorium where a multi-media program orients visitors to the displays. The Sea Shop, located just off the foyer, may be entered before going into the main exhibit areas.

Exhibits

The Galleries

Lining the main galleries, 133 exhibit tanks containing fresh or salt water are maintained at three different temperatures — tropical, temperate or cold — to house the inhabitants of the world's oceans and lakes. Each water system is indicated on eye-level signs at the entrance to every gallery, and is also designated on the floor plan.

All exhibits are on the main floor

Galleries 4, 5, 6 and Tributaries display freshwater animals from lakes, rivers and streams throughout the world.

Galleries 1, 2 and 3, the Coral Reef, Sea Anemone Exhibit and Marine Jewels feature saltwater animals from all oceans.

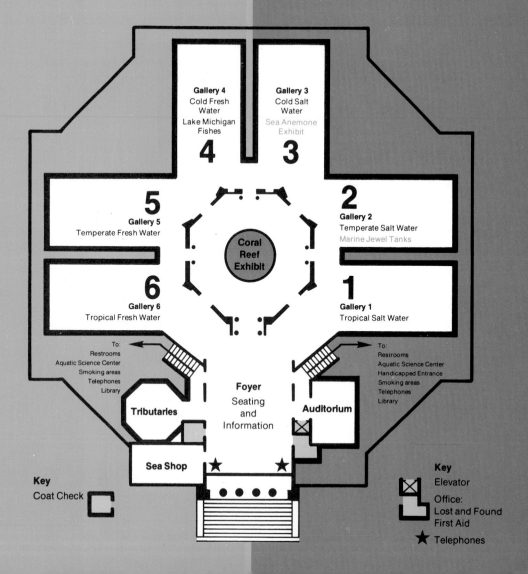

Gallery 4
Cold Fresh Water
Lake Michigan Fishes

4

Gallery 3
Cold Salt Water
Sea Anemone Exhibit

3

5

Gallery 5
Temperate Fresh Water

2

Gallery 2
Temperate Salt Water
Marine Jewel Tanks

Coral Reef Exhibit

6

Gallery 6
Tropical Fresh Water

1

Gallery 1
Tropical Salt Water

To:
Restrooms
Aquatic Science Center
Smoking areas
Telephones
Library

To:
Restrooms
Aquatic Science Center
Handicapped Entrance
Smoking areas
Telephones
Library

Foyer
Seating and Information

Tributaries

Auditorium

Sea Shop

Key
Coat Check

Key
Elevator
Office:
Lost and Found
First Aid
★ Telephones

Water covers 70 per cent of the earth, and animals thrive in nearly every part of it, whether icy polar seas, steamy tropical pools or clear, cool lakes.

Aquarium displays recreate many of these underwater habitats to best illustrate the tremendous range of aquatic adaptations.

Coral reef, Philippines   Rocky shore, Mexico

Gallery 1 houses brilliantly patterned fish from tropical oceans, in addition to those from mangrove and turtle grass habitats.

Animals from sunlit coral reefs in the Indo-Pacific and other shallow oceans appear in **Gallery 2.**

Cold ocean tidepools and bays and their associated animals are exhibited in **Gallery 3.**

Gallery 4 illustrates a cold freshwater area, the Great Lakes region.

Shallow rivers and warm lakes are the natural habitats of the animals in **Gallery 5.**

Asian, African and South American animals from tropical lakes and rivers appear in **Gallery 6.**

Mountain stream, Montana   Wetlands, Maine

Special permanent exhibits:

Tributaries

Small streams feeding larger, tropical rivers are the natural habitats of animals in this separate exhibit hall. Many of these freshwater displays feature popular home aquarium species. The elegant oriental motif symbolizes the origins of the art of fishkeeping in China more than 2,000 years ago.

Marine Jewels

These smaller, free-standing exhibits in Gallery 2 showcase unusual adaptations that might otherwise be overlooked.

Sea Anemones

Frequently mistaken for "flowers" of the sea, anemones are animals closely related to corals and jellyfish. The John Woodworth Leslie Sea Anemone Exhibit in Gallery 3 displays an assortment of anemones, their relatives and symbiotic associates.

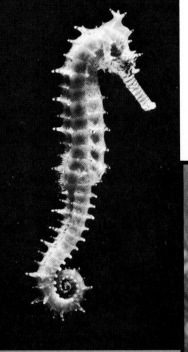

Seahorse
Hippocampus sp.

Anemonefish *Amphiprion ocellaris*,
in carpet anemone, *Stoichactis* sp.

Coral Reef Exhibit

A coral reef is an intricate aquatic community of plants and animals, found only in warm, shallow, sunlit seas. Live, reef-building corals are difficult to maintain in aquariums.

A typical, Caribbean coral reef community is represented in the Coral Reef Exhibit, completed in 1971. It took $1.2 million and more than two years to create the variety of reef habitats that house over 500 tropical fish. The lights go on and off throughout the day in the naturalistic display to simulate the day-night cycle.

The life-like artificial corals in the reef are sculpted or cast in fiberglass with epoxy resins to create realistic formations, such as extensive elkhorn coral or clumps of pillar corals.

A computerized console in the basement controls the water quality and hourly circulation of 90,000 gallons of sea water.

Diver hand-feeding moray eel in the Coral Reef Exhibit

During daily feedings, a diver enters the exhibit and talks to visitors through a microphone in the dive mask while nurse sharks, sea turtles and eels swim by.

Forty feet across, the reef slopes from 8 feet near the windows to 12 feet in the center. The 2¼-inch glass is triple laminated.

Exhibit Information

Information about the exhibits is found on eye-level, back-lit signs that describe tank contents or explain community habitats, and in the **Aquatic Life** section of this guide. To find the appropriate page, look for the animal's common or scientific name in the index.

Interpretive sign

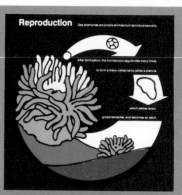

Identification sign

family name:
genus and species name:
common name:

Overhead signs identify an animal through photographs and list the family name first, then its genus and species, followed by its common name. Common names may vary according to local usage, and the same common name may be used for several different species. For example, dogfish may apply to several species of small sharks or to a freshwater fish, *Amia calva,* known also as bowfin. However, each fish has only one scientific name.

Scientists group living things according to common features that set them apart from all other animals. Each group is assigned a unique name, one that often translates from Greek or Latin to describe a special characteristic.

Archerfish, for example, belong to the genus *Toxotes.* It means "bow-man," referring to their ability to rapidly spit a series of water drops at insects on overhanging plants, knocking them into the water.

Exhibit Animals

Throughout the world's oceans and lakes, it is estimated
that there are more than 20,000 known species of fish, in
addition to other animals that live in water —
invertebrates, mammals, birds and reptiles. Many of
these are exceedingly rare, or are impossible to secure
and keep alive in an aquarium.

The natural life span of fishes varies greatly with the
different species. Some specimens live for 50 or more
years in captivity, for example, the Australian lungfish,
page 72, and the tarpon, page 83. Others never survive
more than a few weeks and thus are purposely excluded
from acquisition lists.

Not all of the animals described in the **Aquatic Life**
section will be on exhibit at any one time, nor will all the
species exhibited always be found in this guide. Every
attempt has been made to include representative
families or species.

Aquatic Life

Aquatic Adaptations

Balloonfish, *Diodon holocanthus,* inflated and at rest.

Water is denser than air. It makes movement more difficult. Vision is limited, and sounds and vibrations travel faster and farther. Odors and tastes diffuse more slowly.

Fishes have evolved an array of bizarre adaptations to these conditions. Among other things, they breathe air, walk, glide, crawl, bear live young, live on and off each other, emit light and display a fantastic range of colors and patterns.

Not only fishes, but invertebrates, mammals, reptiles and birds live in water and may exhibit many of the same adaptations. Amphibians, too, share the watery world but remain closely tied to land.

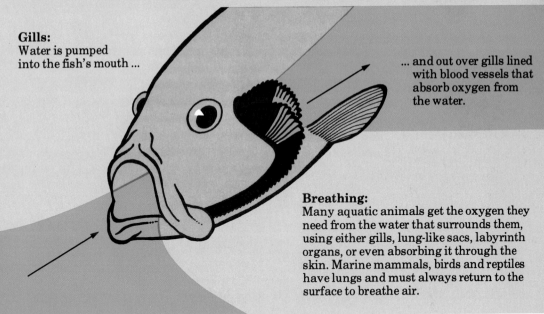

Gills:
Water is pumped
into the fish's mouth ...

... and out over gills lined
with blood vessels that
absorb oxygen from
the water.

Breathing:
Many aquatic animals get the oxygen they
need from the water that surrounds them,
using either gills, lung-like sacs, labyrinth
organs, or even absorbing it through the
skin. Marine mammals, birds and reptiles
have lungs and must always return to the
surface to breathe air.

Range of Fish Senses

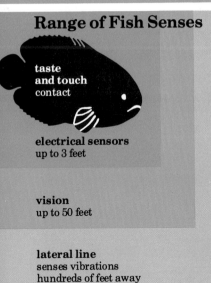

**taste
and touch**
contact

electrical sensors
up to 3 feet

vision
up to 50 feet

lateral line
senses vibrations
hundreds of feet away

smell
up to several hundred yards

Senses:
Fishes generally have excellent senses of
hearing and smell, and depend less on
eyesight. Their more specialized senses
include the lateral line, electrical sensors
and barbels near the mouth that "taste"
when dragged along the bottom.

The lateral line is a long-distance sense
of touch. Fluid-filled pits in the skin
contain hair-like threads. These pick up
vibrations caused by objects disturbing
the water, such as a neighboring fish in a
school.

A few fishes emit and receive their own
electrical impulses to help them navigate
in murky water, find food and, in a few
cases, to stun prey.

hearing
up to several thousand yards

Shape:
It suggests where an animal lives and how it moves.

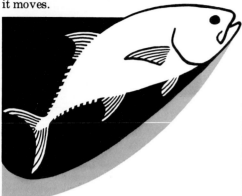

Streamlined bodies move quickly through open water.

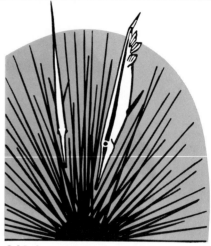

Odd-shaped fish often hide in unusual places.

Long, skinny eels lurk in cracks and crevices.

Thin, flat fish usually live on the bottom.

Coral crab

Some animals never leave the bottom, crawling to find food or shelter.

Movement:
Many fishes and a few other aquatic animals swim by moving their tails from side to side. Others "walk" or "glide" on modified fins, hitchhike, or sit still, like anemones, rarely or never moving. Penguins "fly" underwater using paddle-like wings, moving fast enough to catch fish.

Color:

Animals of the open seas or lakes are often silver. Those that live on the bottom usually match their surroundings.

Colors can be a warning that a fish is venomous,

Lionfish

Harlequin tuskfish

...signal territoriality or a combative nature,

...or advertise a cleaning service.

Cleaner wrasse on a yellow tang.

Humped scorpionfish

Color, combined with shape, may hide a hunter or the hunted through camouflage

Whitespeckled moray eel and mimic roundhead

...or confuse predators by mimicking a more dangerous animal.

Transparency offers concealment against almost any background.

Glass catfish

False eye spots and dark bars confuse predators.

Blueback butterflyfish

Feeding:

Mouths tell where an animal lives and how it feeds by

...seizing other animals,

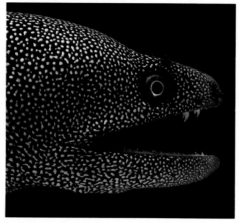

Goldentail moray eel

Arawana

...swallowing meals whole at the surface,

...slurping food off the bottom,

Brown bullhead

Longsnout butterflyfish

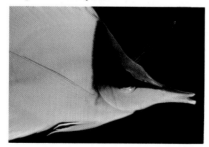

...nibbling tiny plants and animals,

...scraping food off rocks,

Royal plecostomus

Juvenile paddlefish

or filtering plankton from the water.

Juvenile coral catfish

Schooling:
Fish form large groups with others of the same age and species. As they swirl through their aquatic ballet, they find safety in numbers and many opportunities to mate.

Reproduction:
Many aquatic animals lay eggs, sometimes thousands, leaving their survival to chance. Those that lay fewer eggs guard them closely, often building nests. Others protect their young by carrying them in their mouths.

Some fish bear live young and, like male seahorses, may share brooding responsibilities.

Marine mammals give birth to live young at sea or on land, while penguins incubate eggs in crowded rookeries on shore.

3-month-old Peruvian penguin

Harlequin cichlid with young

Aquatic Plants

Eight-foot-long tube worms, *Riftia pachyptila*, are among the unusual organisms recently found close to a warm-water vent near the Galapagos rift, over 8,000 feet deep.

Green plants are the ultimate source of food, the organic energy that sustains all life on earth. They contain chlorophyll and other pigments in highly intricate structures that convert light energy from the sun into chemical energy. This energy binds simple substances into the complex organic molecules that make up all living things.

A few other organisms produce their own food, but these play only a minor role in supporting the vast majority of life. Most notable of these are bacteria recently discovered living in deep marine trenches near the Galapagos. These bacteria convert chemical energy from volcanic rifts into organic energy that supports oases of life in those lightless regions.

Blue-green Algae

Division Cyanochloronta

The blue-green algae are an important component of freshwater and marine phytoplankton (plant plankton) communities. They also grow in sheets or filaments attached to rocks and other substrates in fresh, marine and brackish waters. They are often involved in algal blooms — explosive growths in waters polluted with too many nutrients. Some species produce toxins, which can kill fishes and other animals where algal growth is heavy. Bluish pigments along with green chlorophyll give blue-green algae their name. Yet, as is often the case, common names can be misleading and some blue-green algae are actually red in color. The Red Sea may have gotten its name from one such species, which tints the water when it blooms.

Green Algae
Division Chlorophycophyta

This major group of algae occurs in a wide range of aquatic habitats in both planktonic and attached forms. Green mats of algae can be seen growing on the rocks and walls of most of the Aquarium's displays. On sunny days or in well-lit exhibits, these mats glisten with thousands of tiny oxygen bubbles — a by-product of photosynthesis.

As they grow, algae assimilate fish wastes and other contaminants in the water. They therefore help to maintain water quality in aquariums. Filters, designed to grow large numbers of algae, are established behind the scenes at the Aquarium for this purpose.

Many green algae grow in a more "plant-like" form. Sea lettuce, *Ulva,* has leafy blades like the vegetable and

Sea lettuce
Ulva sp.

Calcareous green algae
Halimeda incrassata

Grape algae
Caulerpa racemosa

is also edible. *Caulerpa racemosa,* found in the Caribbean, looks like clusters of small green grapes. The fern-like blades of *Caulerpa sertularioides* can sometimes be seen in the Marine Jewel Tanks.

Members of the tropical genus *Halimeda* deposit calcium carbonate in their tissues, giving them a hard, crusty texture. Often growing in dense mats, they harbor many species of invertebrates. Their limestone remains contribute to the build-up of reefs, especially in deeper water where reef-building corals cannot survive.

Brown Algae

Division Phaeophycophyta

The brown algae are a marine group, many of which grow in large branching forms and are commonly called seaweeds. They anchor themselves to rocks with holdfasts, structures often mistaken for roots.

The most familiar brown algae are the fast-growing kelp. Some species grow to lengths of over 100 feet. Abundant on the west coast of North America, kelp form important communities. Many animals find food and security among these dense kelp "forests." A replica of such a community is displayed in Gallery 3.

Kelp
Macrocystis

Kelp are used as food and are also fed to livestock in some areas. They are harvested for a substance called algin, which is used in making ice cream, cosmetics and pharmaceutical products.

Sargassum weed, *Sargassum natans,* another type of brown algae, is a floating species found in the "Sargasso Sea," an area in the North Atlantic from the Bahamas to the Azores. Patches of sargassum weed can be found drifting in currents off the Florida Keys. A unique and

Various algae at low tide.

specialized community of small animals has become adapted to life amidst these intertwining algal mats. Small fishes seek refuge there and are followed by larger fishes looking for food.

Other brown algae, such as rockweeds, *Fucus,* and bladderwracks, *Ascophyllum,* are common in cold and temperate coastal waters, growing in great masses attached to rocks. Most reach lengths of one to three feet and have buoyant air bladders that support them in the water. Intertidal species are exposed to the air at low tide. Crabs, snails and other animals stay moist and protected beneath this dense cover during these periods.

Diatoms

Division Chrysophycophyta

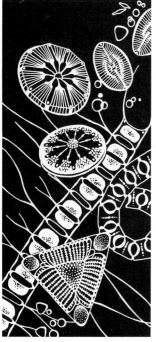

An assortment of diatoms

Diatoms inhabit both fresh and marine habitats and are the most abundant of the world's plants. A gallon of ocean water may contain two million of these tiny, planktonic algae. Diatoms and other planktonic algae are known as phytoplankton. It has been estimated that 25 per cent of the world's plant production is accomplished by diatoms. Sometimes called the "pastures of the seas," these tiny plants are food for myriad microscopic animals, zooplankton, that are in turn eaten by larger animals. Diatoms are thus the base of complex food webs that fuel many marine ecosystems. They are also important producers of oxygen.

Diatoms are encased by two-valved, glassy shells that are often beautifully formed with lacy patterns, rays and beads. The shells sink to the sea floor when the diatoms die, forming thick deposits that are mined for a variety of uses. Diatomaceous earth is used at the Aquarium as a filtering medium. The fine, mesh-like structures trap minute particles, leaving the water crystal clear.

Red Algae

Division Rhodophycophyta

Red algae, like brown algae, are often called seaweeds. They grow in a variety of forms; leafy, brushy, wiry and branching species are common. Many are not reddish at all, and members of this group exhibit a wide range of colors. Red algae seldom grow larger than three feet long. They are most common in tropical seas, but there are many cool-water species as well. Two of these, laver, *Porphyra,* and Irish moss, *Chondrus crispus,* are familiar to those who explore Atlantic tidepools. Both species are used for food, and Irish moss is harvested for making gels and other industrial products.

Red algae can grow under low light levels, enabling them to survive at greater depths than other algae. The coralline red algae, *Corallinaceae,* concentrate calcium carbonate in their tissues and form reefs in some areas. They are remarkable for their ability to survive cold temperatures and great depths.

Sea Grasses

Relatively few flowering plants are able to survive in salt water. Those that do often form communities of great importance to marine life. Among these, a variety of marine "grasses," such as eelgrass, turtlegrass and sea grass, grow in shallow, inshore areas and protected flats behind coral reefs. They are named for their flat, blade-like leaves, yet are not true grasses.

Grass beds provide food for grazing animals, such as snails, sea urchins and some sea turtles. Sponges, hydroids and algae attach themselves to the blades while burrowing worms, shrimps and clams live among the roots. Many reef fishes spawn in nearby grass beds where the young find small food items abundant. Grunts, snappers and other predators are also attracted to these rich areas.

True grasses, such as salt cordgrasses, *Spartina,* grow in lush intertidal meadows, especially along the east coast of North America. Salt marshes are extremely productive and have a diversity of associated animal life. Offshore fishes use the marshes as nurseries. Tremendous numbers of plankton, living off nutrients created by the grasses, are in turn eaten by the young fish.

Turtlegrass bed, *Thalassia testudinum,* surrounding a dead coral head.

Mangroves

Mangroves are salt-tolerant trees that grow along tropical coasts. Naturalist Annie Dillard describes them as "...short, messy trees, waxy-leaved, laced all over with aerial roots, woody arching buttresses, and weird leathery berry pads. All this tangles from a black muck soil...." Not all of the trees fit this description, for "mangrove" is a collective term applied to a variety of species from several different families.

Waxy mangrove leaves retain water while exuding salt to keep the tissues from becoming too salty. Some species solve this problem by preventing the salt from being taken up by the roots. The knobby tangle of aerial roots allows oxygen transfer and helps trap debris that forms a rich, mucky soil.

Mangroves fuel a rich and diverse community. Bacteria living in the muck decompose fallen mangrove leaves. This releases nutrients utilized by dense populations of small invertebrates. These in turn are preyed upon by other animals, including those that live attached to the roots.

Starfish, shrimps and snails find food and safety among the mangroves. Fishes patrol the channels and edges of mangrove swamps, living off the complex invertebrate and fish communities found there.

Mangroves
Rhizophora mangle

Other communities reap the benefits of the mangroves' bounty. Many reef fishes use the mangroves as a nursery. Their fry thrive on small invertebrates before migrating to the reef, thus energy captured by the trees flows to offshore habitats.

Mangroves spread by means of their buoyant seed pods. These drop off and float until coming to rest on a site with sufficient soil for them to sprout and grow.

Because their tangled network of roots disperses the force of heavy waves, mangroves are frequently encouraged to grow in some areas to protect coastlines from hurricanes.

Freshwater Plants

Freshwater aquatic plants are displayed in many Aquarium exhibits where they provide the fishes with natural hiding places and areas for spawning. Of the hundreds of species, most commonly seen are the grass-like *Vallisneria* and *Sagittaria,* feathery *Myriophyllum* and the flat-leaved *Cryptocoryne.*

Emergent plants, such as cattails and rushes, root in water but send shoots into the air, and can often be seen in pond habitat displays.

Volo bog

White water lily
Nymphaea odorata

Invertebrates

protists
Protozoa

sponges
Porifera

sea anemones
jelly fish
corals
Cnidaria
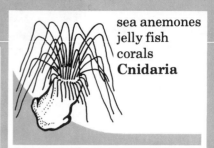

flatworms
Platyhelminthes

This section includes only
those marine invertebrates
likely to be exhibited.

clams
snails
octopuses
Mollusca

worms
Annelida

barnacles
crabs
shrimps
lobsters
Arthropoda

starfish
sea urchins
sea cucumbers
Echinodermata

sea squirts
Chordata

Aquatic invertebrates include some of the most
beautifully colored and delicately constructed life forms
known, exceeding even the fishes in number and variety.

They swarm in countless millions both in fresh and
salt water, feeding on each other or plants and in turn
being preyed upon by practically all other forms of
animal life, including man. While most aquatic
invertebrates are microscopic in size, a few species
attain huge proportions. Many of the larger species are
valuable to man as food.

The Aquarium exhibits several of the more conspicuous
and hardy species. These sea creatures, including sea
anemones, file clams and other exotic invertebrates, thrive
in the Marine Jewels displays and Sea Anemone Exhibit
on a special diet of liquid food and brine shrimp.

Ghost anemone shrimp
Periclemenes pedersoni

One-celled Life

phylum Protozoa

Too small to display, the nearly invisible, single-celled protozoans deserve mention because of their importance to all aquatic life.

Millions of these "first animals" and plants ride the currents of all lakes and seas, forming the essential base of the food web when eaten by tiny animals that in turn feed larger species, and so on.

Some swim by beating the water with hair-like appendages, others have stalks and live permanently attached, while parasites live in or on other plants or animals. A few, the dinoflagellates, make their own food using chloroplasts, the structure all plants use to convert light energy into food. Sudden "blooms" of these tiny marine animals stain coastal waters red, hence the term "red tides." Dense populations are lethal to many fish swimming in the affected waters. Also, shellfish filter these microscopic animals from the water, and during red tides concentrate high levels. The contaminated shellfish become toxic to animals that eat them, including fish, sea birds and people.

Protozoans dazzle the imagination with their variety of shapes and designs. The lime skeletons of some sink to the sea floor. These form thick deposits over thousands of years, such as the white cliffs of Dover, which were exposed by changing sea levels. Others have intricate glass skeletons.

An assortment of protozoans

Sponges

phylum Porifera

"Pore-bearers," or sponges, are among the simplest of animals. They have no true organs or tissues, yet may grow to an astounding six feet in diameter. Hundreds of canals riddle a sponge. Cells lining the canals get food and oxygen from the huge volume of water that passes through. Crabs, shrimps and brittle stars sometimes seek shelter within the maze of pores, converting sponges into veritable condominiums.

Live sponges are seldom displayed. Exhibits contain skeletons of larger forms or hand-sculpted, fiberglass versions of these and encrusting sponges.

In every ocean, at all depths, sponges add reds, oranges, yellows, greens, blues, purples and black to the underwater landscape. A few live in some freshwater lakes and rivers. The more than 5,000 species are

Iridescent tube sponge
Spinosella plicifera

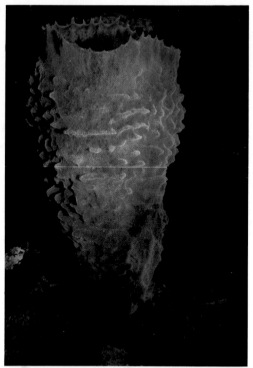

Cross-section
of a typical sponge

A sponge extracts food and oxygen from the vast quantity of sea water that continuously flows through its many canals.

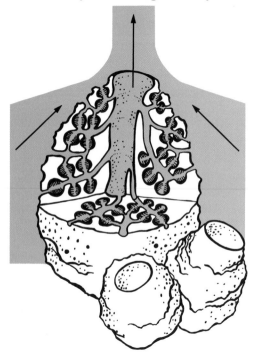

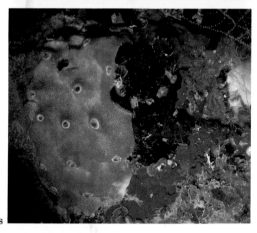

Encrusting sponges

distinguished by the intricate slivers of lime or glass, called spicules, that form their skeletons. Others, such as the familiar bath sponge, are supported by a protein fiber known as spongin, but may also have spicules. Sponge shapes and sizes vary, even within a species, according to the environment. They range from flat, colorful mats in intertidal zones to tall, upright forms in deeper, quiet water. Some resemble vases, balls or fingers and weigh over 200 pounds. Boring sponges tunnel into mollusc shells and corals by means of chemical excavation.

hydroids class **Hydrozoa**	true jellyfish class **Scyphozoa**	corals anemones class **Anthozoa**

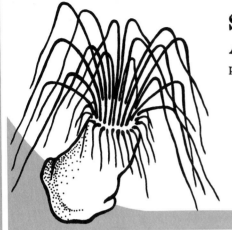

Stinging Animals
phylum Cnidaria

Potent, microscopic stinging capsules (shown before and after firing) line the tentacles of hydroids, jellyfish and sea anemones.

Jellyfish, corals and anemones are cnidarians, "animals that sting." These soft, tube-like animals, bristling with stinging tentacles, capture prey and defend themselves with their unique stinging capsules.

Hydroids

One of the few freshwater hydroids is the inch-long, solitary *Hydra* of North American ponds, lakes, streams and high school biology classes.

Often mistaken for clumps of seaweed, a closer look at a colony of small hydroids, *Tubularia,* reveals many tubular bodies and tentacle-ringed mouths. The attached bases of these small animals are usually connected through a shared "root system." These hydroids reproduce by sending out small forms resembling minute jellyfish, called medusae, that swim to new habitats before attaching to suitable surfaces.

A gigantic relative, by comparison, is the well-known hydroid from the open seas, the purple man-o-war, *Physalia.* Its foot-long, gas-filled violet float drifts on the surface, trailing fish-catching tentacles for 30 feet or more. Armed with potent stinging cells, the tentacles contain a virulent venom that causes severe pain, the resultant shock known to kill people.

The fire coral, *Millepora,* found throughout the West Indies, looks like a true coral. It is really a hydroid colony that secretes a hard lime casing around itself. Careless swimmers and divers who brush against it feel an intense burning sensation.

Colonial hydroids

Fire coral
Millepora

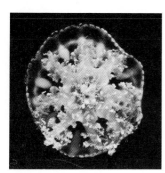

Upside-down jellyfish
Cassiopeia xamachana

Jellyfish

Pulsing, bell-shaped jellyfish sting fish and other prey with their clusters of tentacles. Although most jellyfish are harmless to people, the Pacific sea wasp, *Chironex,* poses a danger to swimmers because of its lethal venom. Dwarfing the one-foot-diameter sea wasp and its other relatives, the immense lion's mane jellyfish, *Cyanea,* grows to over eight feet in diameter and trails tentacles more than 100 feet long.

One of the shallow-water varieties thrives in well-lit aquariums. The tropical, upside-down jellyfish, *Cassiopeia,* common in shallow seas and mangrove swamps, spends the majority of its life lying on the bottom, upside down. Gardens of algae grow within its highly branched tentacles, held up towards the sunlight. The jellyfish may feed on the algae in addition to particles it strains from the water.

Corals, anemones and relatives

Corals and anemones decorate the seas in a profusion of colors and forms. This beautiful and diverse group includes hard and soft corals, sea whips and fans, sea pens, zoanthids and false corals as well as sea anemones and tube anemones.

Elkhorn coral
Acropora palmata

Pillar coral
Dendrogyra cylindrus

Caribbean coral reef

Many of the hard or stony true corals form intricate reef communities in sunlit, tropical shallows. Perhaps the most famous is the 1,200-mile Great Barrier Reef, along the northeast coast of Australia. Extensive reefs also occur in the Caribbean and off the coast of Central America.

Reef-building corals create one of the richest marine habitats in a normally unproductive environment. They offer food and protection to thousands of plants and animals, including many commercially valuable species.

Most stony corals live in colonies, consisting of many minute, interconnected individuals. Each soft coral animal, or polyp, secretes a hard casing of lime around itself. It pokes out at night to feed, retreating if threatened by coral-eating fishes. Hundreds of millions of tiny coral polyps often create massive, branching forms. A Caribbean elkhorn coral, *Acropora palmata,* the size of the one represented in the Coral Reef Exhibit, would contain about 250 coral polyps per square inch.

Reef-building corals require vast amounts of sunlight and clear, warm sea water. Because tropical waters are relatively barren, corals survive by feeding in several ways. They catch tiny animals, absorb dissolved organic matter and get food from the gardens of algae that grow in their own soft bodies. Because these algae, called zooxanthallae, require sunlight, the depth at which these corals grow is limited. Deepwater corals are not the reef-building variety. Although corals are difficult to keep alive in aquariums, their skeletons provide natural habitats for a wide array of reef animals in most of the saltwater displays. Many of the colorful varieties are represented by hand-sculpted, artificial corals.

Unlike their stony relatives, the brightly colored soft corals sway and wave in the ocean currents as they trap food.

Those in another closely related group, the sea feathers, whips and fans, stand upright, supported by branching skeletons made of a horny material, gorgonin. Among these, one is highly prized. The precious red coral, *Corallium rubrum,* of the Mediterranean, is polished and carved into jewelry.

Sea pens resemble antique quill pens, buried point first into the ocean bottom. Heart-shaped sea pansies, on the other hand, slowly creep along the shallow, sandy sea floor at night, polyps exposed, searching for fine particles of food. Both sea pens and pansies flash with bioluminescence when disturbed at night.

Reef-building corals

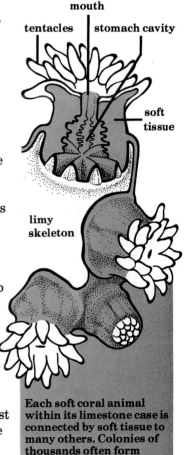

Each soft coral animal within its limestone case is connected by soft tissue to many others. Colonies of thousands often form intricate or massive structures such as elkhorn and pillar corals.

Common sea fan
Gorgonia ventalina

Zoanthids

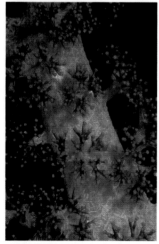

Soft coral

The zoanthids are tiny, anemone-like animals. Colonies form dense mats in shallow, tropical seas on reefs, or just below the low tide mark. A few live in cold water or at great depths.

False corals resemble anemones externally. They resemble true corals in many less visible ways. In some, the club-tipped tentacles are no more than nubby growths near the mouth.

Mistaken for flowers, brightly colored sea anemones display blossoms of petal-like tentacles, but are animals, not plants. The order name, Actiniaria, means "flower animals." Anemones range from less than a half inch to nearly six feet in diameter, the largest being the tropical Pacific *Stoichactis* species, known as carpet anemones.

Anemones feed on other animals. Those with stout, well-developed tentacles catch small fishes and active crustaceans. Others, such as the coldwater feeble anemone, *Metridium,* trap and sting tiny animals in their plumes of feathery tentacles.

Many sea anemones firmly fasten onto rocks with their adhesive bases, even in wave-tossed tidal areas. Not all remain attached. Some somersault away from danger, others glide, while a few hitchhike on the backs of hermit crabs, or other animals. Several anemones burrow for protection.

Anemones reproduce sexually or by splitting down the middle lengthwise into two anemones. Tiny buds appearing on the bases of some anemones later sprout tentacles to become complete, miniature versions of the parent.

Many anemones share "mutual admiration societies" with a wide variety of fishes and invertebrates. Hermit crabs carry the hitchhiker anemone, *Calliactis,* on their shells as a defense against predators that will avoid the anemone's bristling tentacles. One small crab, *Lybia,* carries a tiny anemone on each claw, earning the name "pom pom" crab. It waves its well-armed claws in the face of a predator to discourage an attack, and in doing so resembles an enthusiastic cheerleader.

Many small animals seek protection from enemies by living, unharmed, among an anemone's tentacles. Cleaner shrimps dwell there, as do tiny porcelain crabs.

The best known of all the symbiotic relationships occurs between large tropical anemones, such as *Radianthus* and *Stoichactis,* and the several dozen species of anemonefishes of the genera *Amphiprion* and *Premnas.* The red, orange and white fish wriggle through the tentacles in a special dance that eventually allows them to snuggle into the venomous tentacles without being stung and paralyzed. In return, they

Mediterranean tube anemone
Cerianthus membranaceus

Giant green anemone
Anthopleura xanthogrammica

Feeble anemone
Metridium senile

Sea anemones, or "flower animals," catch live food in their stinging tentacles, which number from eight to many thousands. The tentacles then fold inward, carrying food to the central mouth and stomach.

Cross-section of a typical sea anemone

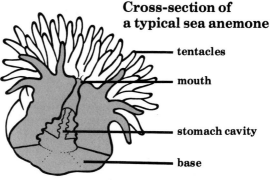

— tentacles

— mouth

— stomach cavity

— base

occasionally bring the anemone a morsel of food, remove debris or perhaps attract a victim to within reach of the anemone's deadly stinging cells.

Tube anemones, closely related to sea anemones, make their own shelters. A tube anemone accumulates sand and mud on the mucus it secretes, forming an upright, leathery tube. Waving from the top of a tube as long as three feet, slender tentacles trap small fish and crustaceans.

Flatworms
phylum Platyhelminthes

The elegantly ruffled, gaudily colored flatworms common to tropical reefs are surprisingly related to the dread tapeworm and tiny flukes that parasitize fishes.

Seldom exhibited, the beautiful, ocean-dwelling flatworms usually feed at night on hydroids, tunicates and other animals, or scavenge. More secretive varieties, often less than half an inch long, seek cover or live buried in the bottom.

One well-known flatworm, the freshwater *Dugesia*, has the remarkable ability to grow back into a complete animal from tiny pieces. More impressive, perhaps, are the simple behaviors it learns and remembers with its primitive brain, running a maze for food, for example.

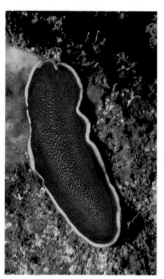

Purple flatworm
Pseudoceros sp.

Segmented Worms
phylum Annelida

The well-known earthworm has many relatives that live submerged in seas, rivers and lakes worldwide. Segmented worms common to aquatic habitats include the notorious bloodsucking leeches, bristle worms and beautiful feather dusters.

Leeches live as parasites in both fresh and salt water, attaching to turtles, wading birds, mammals, skates and rays as well as fishes. Their former medicinal use as blood-drainers is well documented. Others are carnivores that feed on worms and small invertebrates. Some eat plants.

Most numerous of all the marine worms, the segmented worms known as polychaetes occupy a variety of habitats from intertidal regions to the greatest depths. Ranging in size from a quarter inch to over nine feet in length, most hide in crevices, sponges, in the sand, or build their own limestone or leathery tube shelters. Some hide in holes bored into coral heads.

Bristle worms crawl freely along the bottom, feeding voraciously on smaller animals, or sea whips and fans. Their name alone should warn the unwary beachcomber tempted to pick up for closer examination a brightly colored green bristle worm, *Hermodice,* or orange bristle worm, *Eurythoe.* The easily shed bristles, finer than cactus spines, penetrate even the toughest, calloused skin, causing excruciating pain, swelling and tenderness that last for weeks.

The more beautiful fan or feather duster worms tentatively peek from leathery looking tubes the worm secretes as it grows. The delicate plume "feathers" are really gills that get oxygen as well as filter tiny food particles from the water. When disturbed, the worm quickly withdraws.

Spiral, double-crowned Christmas tree tube worms, *Spirobranchus giganteus,* build a harder, limestone tube. At the first threat of danger, the crown disappears into the protective tube with lightning-quick speed, and a "plug" seals the delicate plumes safely inside. These tube worms often form colonies, building upon each others' tubes. Worm reefs can be a locally significant feature in warm, shallow waters, and offer protection for fishes and other invertebrates.

Sabellid fan worms

Fire bristle worm, *Hermodice carunculata,* feeding on a sea whip.

snails
conchs
cowries
class **Gastropoda**

chitons
class **Polyplacopha**

clams
oysters
mussels
class **Bivalvia**

octopuses
squids
nautiluses
class **Cephalopoda**

Soft-bodied Animals
phylum Mollusca

Snails, clams, octopuses and squids are among over 100,000 species of molluscs that flourish in rivers, lakes and oceans worldwide, the majority inhabiting warm, shallow seas. Well known for their hard shells, only a few are shell-less, such as the beautiful nudibranchs and fast-swimming octopuses and squids.

Chitons
The oval, eight-plated shell of a chiton, or "sea cradle," is known from the surf zones of all oceans. The shell covers an extremely large, muscular foot that clings tightly to wave-washed rocks exposed by the tides. At night, most move slowly while grazing on algae from the rocks. Afterwards, they often return to the same spot where they remain stationary during the day. Chitons range in size from one inch to one foot in length.

Squiggled chitons
Tonicella lineata

Snails
A snail's stomach is surrounded by the prominent foot on which it glides, hence the group's name, Gastropoda, or "stomach-footed."

When in danger, the slow-moving snail withdraws its muscular foot into a spiraling, one-room shelter of diverse shape and design. Shell collectors treasure the glossy, multi-patterned shells of the cowrie and cone snail, or the larger, pink-tinted conch. Some are also harvested for their tasty flesh. Conch meat flavors the popular tropical chowders. The succulent abalone brings a high price on the West Coast.

Feeding habits among snails vary. The marine periwinkle, *Littorina littorea,* and many freshwater snails scrape algae from rocks with their rough, stiffened tongues. The latter graze in many of the freshwater displays, keeping them clean.

The queen conch, *Strombus gigas,* of the Caribbean, specializes in feeding on small algae growing on turtle grass. Its names allude to its giant, spiral shell that measures up to 12 inches long. One of the conch's chief predators is the larger, carnivorous tulip snail, *Pleuroploca gigantea,* known as the horse conch. At 18 inches, it is one of the largest snails.

Florida fighting conch
Strombus alatus

The beautiful, gentle cowries, *Cypraea,* graze on soft corals and hydroids. By contrast, the cone snails, *Conus,* harpoon other snails or small fish with their long venomous tongues. Six species are dangerous to man, attacks proving fatal 25 per cent of the time.

Many of the graceful, beautiful shell-less nudibranchs, or sea slugs, feed unharmed on stinging sea anemones and hydroids. Several varieties swallow the stinging cells without triggering the firing mechanism, attaching them to their backs to discourage predators. Many are unpalatable or produce toxins, their bold colors warning of an unpleasant taste.

Deer cowrie
Cypraea cervus

Limpets, *Acmaea,* graze by the hundreds on algae-covered rocks in the intertidal zone. Sheltered within a dome-shaped shell that resembles a small volcano, a limpet withstands pounding waves by clamping firmly onto the rocks with a large foot.

Clams, Oysters and Mussels

Tasty, commercially valuable clams, oysters and their bivalve relatives hold two shells together with powerful muscles, extending only a single, hatchet-shaped foot to burrow in the sand, or to move slowly over the bottom. Those with a poorly developed foot — mussels, for example — live a stationary life, firmly attaching themselves with strong, yet flexible threads called byssi. By contrast, scallops swim short distances by snapping their shells open and shut, castanet-style.

Many bivalves filter food from water pumped through their partially open shells. Long-necked siphons protrude from the burrows of those that hide in the sand. Others dredge up bottom sediments, digesting the edible portions. A specialized clam, the teredo or shipworm, eats wood as it bores through submerged structures, such as boats, docks, etc.

The smallest bivalves measure less than a half inch, while the legendary giant *Tridacna* clam of the South Pacific may grow to over four feet across and weigh up to

Fishing-
decoy mussel
Lampsilis ovata

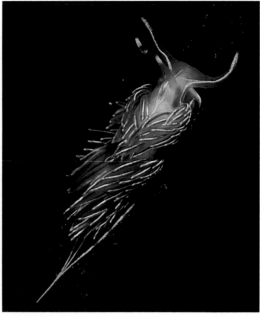

Goldtipped nudibranch
Asteronotus brassica

Least tridacna clam
Tridacna crocea

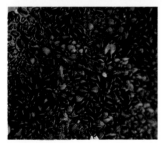

Edible mussels
Mytilus edulis

500 pounds. Bearing false reputations as man-eaters, these harmless molluscs close their shells tightly to protect soft bodies, but almost too slowly to trap a diver's misplaced arms or legs. Giant clams are filter feeders, and also cultivate gardens of algae in their mantles. The algae produce sugars and oxygen the clam can use.

Clams and most bivalves usually release clouds of millions of larvae that are dispersed by the currents. However, the young of certain freshwater clams develop on host fish while hitchhiking to new territory. The fishing-decoy mussel, *Lampsilis,* attracts host fish with a small lure, complete with fins, tail and eyespot formed from its own fleshy mantle. As this decoy fish wiggles in the current, a would-be-predator approaches, only to be surrounded by a swarm of larval clams that attach to the inquisitive fish.

Octopuses, Nautiluses, Squids, Cuttlefishes
Octopuses and their relatives bear little resemblance to other molluscs. Called "head-footed" animals, or cephalopods, their many tentacles attach directly to their fleshy heads. Only the nautilus retains a magnificent shell. The squid and cuttlefish carry small remnants inside, while the octopus has no trace of a shell.

Briar octopus
Octopus briareus

Octopuses

Octopods, octopuses and octopi are all correct references
to these famous, eight-armed molluscs. They are found
in cold, warm and tropical oceans from the tidal zone to
depths of over three miles. The smallest measures a mere
two inches while the largest species, the giant Pacific
octopus, *Octopus dofleini,* exceeds 32 feet from arm-tip to
arm-tip.

The only hard part of the shell-less octopus is its
parrot-like beak, used to tear apart fish or crush hard-
shelled crabs, shrimp, lobsters, snails and clams. Some
octopuses possess a venom in their saliva capable of
stunning or killing prey. Although octopuses rarely bite
people, an Australian swimmer died within two hours of
being bitten by a six-inch, blue-ringed octopus. Most
octopus venom is less potent.

Powerful suction discs line each tentacle, and help a
night-hunting octopus pull firmly attached shellfish
from rocks.

Normally secretive and shy, octopuses slip through
rock crevices and other hiding places very quickly. This
enables them to flee from enemies, including moray eels.
In open water, octopuses hug their tentacles together
and jet propel backwards at speeds up to eight miles per
hour. A cornered octopus eludes its predators by
squirting a possibly distasteful ink that retains an
octopus-like, torpedo shape, while the octopus changes
color and direction. By the time the confused predator
recovers its senses, the octopus has vanished. Whether
swimming or crawling over the bottom, octopuses
constantly flash many colors and patterns to blend in
instantly with their surroundings.

After an elaborate courtship, the female lays clusters of hundreds of eggs inside her den, closely guarding them until they hatch. Afterwards, she dies. Life spans among the species range from one to three years.

Nautiluses

Found only in the deep waters of the western Pacific, the several known species of nautilus dwell within distinctive, chambered shells. The nautilus continually adds rooms as it grows, living in the outermost of the spiralling chambers. When alarmed, it withdraws its dozens of tentacles and covers the opening with a leathery hood.

The nautilus lives in the largest, outermost chamber and maintains its buoyancy by regulating the amount of gas in the smaller chambers. A tube called a siphuncle connects the spiralling compartments.

The nautilus maintains its buoyancy, despite the heavy shell, by regulating the amount of gas in its various chambers. This slow procedure takes days. A nautilus does not make nightly migrations to within a hundred feet of the surface, as once thought. It moves its bulky shell in other directions very slowly, using the same jet propulsion that carries the more streamlined octopus and squid at higher speed.

Scavenging on the bottom for lobsters or crabs, the nautilus' many tentacles, lined with suckers, seize food and carry it to its beak-like mouth.

Squids

The torpedo-shaped squids catch prey with their ten tentacles, two of which are much longer than the rest.

The smaller species cruise the open seas in huge schools and rarely survive in confined spaces. Thousands of pounds of squid are fed to exhibit animals here yearly.

The legendary giant squid pits its 50-foot length against sperm whales that hunt them in the oceans' depths. What little else is known about these solitary giants has been learned from the few specimens that have washed ashore.

Both the high-speed squids and cuttlefish swim faster than 16 miles an hour, or may hover motionless over the bottom.

False cuttlefish squid
Sepioteuthis sepioidea

Cuttlefishes

The more sedate cuttlefish often acclimate well to aquariums. One cuttlefish, *Sepia*, catches a variety of fishes and invertebrates by lying motionless on the bottom, changing shape and color to camouflage itself, and then suddenly pouncing on a crab or shrimp that wanders too close.

Bird fanciers often give their pets the cuttlefish's internal support, a large "cuttlebone," for sharpening their beaks.

Cuttlefish
Sepia sp.

| aquatic insects
class **Insecta** | horseshoe crabs
class **Merostomata** | copepods
class **Copepoda** |

Joint-legged Animals
phylum Arthropoda

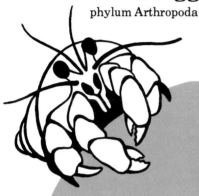

barnacles
class **Cirripedia**

mantis shrimps
krill
shrimps
lobsters
crabs
class **Malacostraca**

Crabs, shrimps, lobsters and their relatives have jointed legs and rigid skeletons that must be shed for the animal to grow, a process that exposes the animal's soft body for a day or two until a new, larger shell hardens.

One of the most commercially valuable groups to man, it contains over three-quarters of all known species of animal life, more than 750,000. The majority of these belong to the various groups of insects, many of which have aquatic stages in their development.

Aquatic Insects
Numerous species of insects have adapted to life in or on water. They occur in every freshwater habitat, as well as in salt water. Their importance as food for aquatic animals cannot be exaggerated. Many fishes, amphibians, shorebirds and waterfowl depend on both the submerged and terrestrial stages of these insects.

A few, in turn, are predators of small fishes and fry, dragonflies, for example, or water bugs and water beetles. Among the latter, the water strider may be the most familiar, visibly skating over the surfaces of ponds and still waters. A covering of many fine hairs or wax prevents their long legs from breaking the surface.

Horseshoe Crabs
Looking more like a two-foot-long, wind-up toy than a diving animal, the armored horseshoe crab jerks along the bottom in shallow oceans or frantically churns the water with flailing legs as it feebly swims short

Submerged dragonfly nymph

Horseshoe crab
Limulus polyphemus

distances. The spike-like tail acts as a lever to right the animal if a wave or its own clumsy swimming lands it in an upside-down position. It sometimes burrows and rests completely buried in the sand.

Mating occurs in large groups in shallow water. The male holds on to the female from behind, often for several days, and occasionally a second male attaches to the first, the procession looking like a string of railroad cars. A few hundred eggs are laid, fertilized and the shallow nest covered with sand before adults depart.

Scientists use the blue, copper-based blood of the horseshoe crab to diagnose certain types of cancer. Inedible, the abundant horseshoe crabs have little commercial value except as fertilizer.

Only four species represent this living relic today, whose nearly identical ancestors flourished in seas millions of years ago. A single species, *Limulus polyphemus,* is found in North America, from Nova Scotia to the Gulf of Mexico.

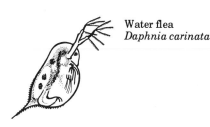

Water flea
Daphnia carinata

Crustaceans
subphylum Crustacea

Crabs, shrimps, crayfishes and lobsters are the most popular and commercially valuable crustaceans, their annual harvest yielding billions of dollars.

Many of the smaller, less well-known species are food for larger animals in the aquatic food chain. Among these, both the freshwater *Daphnia* and miniature brine shrimp, *Artemia,* sustain the smaller exhibit animals. The latter is cultured and fed live to fishes that have special diet requirements.

Copepods
Tiny copepods, less than one-tenth of an inch long, graze on even smaller plants and animals known as phytoplankton. In turn, their profuse numbers become the basic food for many marine and freshwater fishes during some stage of their development. Bottom-dwelling species are known from depths as great as 7,000 feet, while others live as parasites on whales and fishes. Pin-head size dots on the inside walls of exhibit tanks may be copepods, which reproduce readily in the Aquarium's water system.

Brine shrimp
Artemia salina

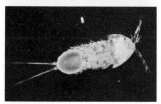

Copepod

Barnacles

Barnacles are the only crustaceans that live cemented in place, sometimes as parasites on sea lilies, brittle stars, starfish, corals and most frequently on shrimps, crabs, lobsters and whales.

The greatest numbers of barnacles occur in the wave-tossed tidal zones of the world's oceans.

The famous naturalist, Louis Agassiz, described a typical barnacle as "nothing more than a little shrimp-like animal, standing on its head in a limestone house and kicking food into its mouth." The long, feathery legs beat in unison, retreating into the shell when they are full of tiny animals. The plated, stony shell bonds to pilings, rocks, whale skin and ships' hulls with the barnacle's own "super glue" of extreme strength. Barnacles are a nuisance to mariners, since a heavy growth on a boat's hull can slow its speed by almost one-third.

Barnacles, *Balanus* sp., on a pier.

Stalked or gooseneck barnacles, *Lepas,* were once thought to be the fruit of the floating trees they colonized, each fruit supposedly developing into a sea bird called the barnacle goose.

Gooseneck barnacles
Lepas sp.

Mantis shrimp

Mantis Shrimps

Named for their resemblance in both appearance and habit to the insect, the praying mantis, these animals range in size from two inches to over one foot. In shallow oceans, they excavate burrows or take advantage of natural crevices. Mantis shrimps feed on invertebrates or fishes by seizing their prey with powerful, lightning-quick thrusts of their razor-sharp front legs.

The mantis shrimp also defends itself with its well-armed claws which have a series of needle-sharp spines on the inner edge. When cornered, it lashes out with these, inflicting painful gashes. Its West Indian name, "thumb-splitter," is well deserved.

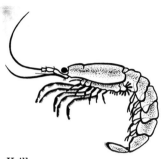

Krill
Euphausia sp.

Krill

Shrimp-like krill live in vast schools in the world's
oceans, from the surface to more than 6,000 feet deep.
Blue whales feed almost exclusively on *Euphausia
superba,* one of 90 species, consuming up to four tons of
the one- to two-inch krill each day. Actively fished by the
Russians and Japanese, krill may some day be an
important food source for many people. Russian trawlers
alone harvested 6,000 tons of krill in 1975. In the
Aquarium, krill supplement many fish diets, but never
appear on exhibit.

Shrimps, Lobsters and Crabs

Shrimps, lobsters and crabs have great commercial
value in the world's seafood industry. Largest of the
crustaceans, they walk or swim with five pairs of legs.
Most of the 8,500 species live in the oceans, a few occur
in fresh water while some of the very specialized crabs
crawl about on land. Diverse in shape, size and habit,
they are known to live at depths as great as 19,000 feet,
and are abundant in open water or in burrows in the
bottom. Many hide in crevices, or inhabit cast-off snail
shells.

The gigantic commercial harvest of edible varieties
encourages fishermen to exploit untapped resources of
deeper water species.

Shrimps

Delicate, candy-striped shrimp are less familiar to most
than the high-priced stars of seafood restaurants. The
succulent, edible shrimp, *Penaeus,* fills the nets of
commercial fishermen in the warm, shallow waters of
the Gulf of Mexico and the eastern United States. These
shrimp burrow in the sand during the day and actively
prowl about at night. They lack the large claws of the
secretive snapping or pistol shrimp, *Alpheus.* When
disturbed, one of the pistol shrimp's large, modified
claws instantly snaps shut, producing a remarkably
loud noise, and its name.

Many species of the one-inch glass shrimp,
Palaemonetes, live in warm, fresh and estuarine waters
throughout the world, as do the large, edible freshwater
prawns. Attempts by aquaculturists to spawn and rear
the commercially valuable giant prawn, *Macro-
brachium,* have met with limited success to date.

The inch-long cleaning shrimps, *Periclimenes,* set up
shop in tropical waters worldwide and are named for
their habit of cleaning parasites and debris from the
skin and teeth of other fishes. They generally advertise
this service with long white antennae atop transparent

bodies marked with bright colors. The two-inch, scarlet cleaner shrimp, *Lysmata grabhami,* carries stripes of gold, red and white. The red-veined cleaning shrimp, *Lysmata wurdemanni,* lacks the typical white antennae of most cleaners. Both shrimps have very fine claws adapted for their delicate task of parasite removal.

The elegant shrimp, *Hymenocera picta,* receives its name from its beautiful patterns and the graceful movements of its legs and claws. Pairs of these inch-long shrimp live together on tropical Indo-Pacific reefs. They feed on starfish and slowly devour their prey, arm by arm, including the crown-of-thorns starfish which decimates coral reefs by eating living coral. A single pair of shrimp can kill a crown-of-thorns more than one hundred times their size within two weeks.

The three-inch long banded coral shrimp, *Stenopus hispidus,* flashes its red and white, barber pole stripes beneath the sign of the cleaner: white antennae. Its large, claw-tipped forearms pick parasites from other animals. Pairs of these tropical shrimp live in reef cracks and crevices or, like other cleaners, often seek shelter near the tentacles of sea anemones, only venturing out when a potential client indicates its sincere desire to be cleaned. Fish signal their sincerity by "dancing" or assuming a certain position.

Ghost anemone shrimp
Periclemenes pedersoni

Elegant shrimp,
Hymenocera picta,
eating a starfish.

Lobsters and Crayfishes

Most popular of the true lobsters is the seafood king, the American lobster, *Homarus americanus.* Found in the cold Atlantic off New England and Canada at depths usually less than 500 feet, the largest known lobsters weigh over 48 pounds. Reports of larger, deepwater animals remain undocumented. The American lobster, like other crustaceans, grows by shedding its crusty, outer shell as many as twelve times in its first year. Older lobsters molt less often, depending on food availability and temperature. Size alone does not reveal a lobster's age, despite stories of large, 100-year-old lobsters.

Lobsters hunt for shellfish, fish and smaller crustaceans at night. The larger of the two claws crushes the hard shells of snails, clams and other lobsters. The second claw tears and picks food apart, including great amounts of algae.

Fishermen harvest hundreds of tons of the valuable American lobsters annually. Average weights of one pound are becoming less common, signs of overfishing. New advances in aquaculture suggest that selective breeding and rearing techniques, while still too expensive, may succeed in the future.

A closely related species, *Homarus gammarus,* occurs off the coast of Europe.

Other types of lobsters include the edible red Norwegian lobster, *Nephrops.* Even smaller, the scarlet reef lobster, *Enoplometopus,* hides out in reefs in the tropical Pacific.

Flattened, clawless, armored bodies hide the legs of the slipper-shaped lobsters, *Scyllarides.* Also called

Serrated slipper lobster
Parribacus antarcticus

American lobster
Homarus americanus

Rock lobster
Panulirus guttatus

Red crayfish

Spanish lobsters or shovel-nosed lobsters, most species occur in shallow, warm water. Large specimens of these slow-moving, secretive lobsters may be commercially fished.

Preferring shallow, tropical and temperate waters, the spiny lobsters, *Panulirus,* lack the large front claws characteristic of their coldwater cousins, the true lobsters. Their stout, spine-studded antennae, often longer than their bodies, ward off enemies.

While spiny lobsters seldom reach the large size of the American lobster, many species grow to more than 10 pounds. Frequent reef inhabitants, they eat anything, usually hunting or scavenging at night, hiding in caves and crevices by day. Seasonally, Florida spiny lobsters, *Panulirus argus,* march off single file into deeper water, possibly a single-minded walk to and from spawning grounds. A commercial and sport fishery exists worldwide for spiny lobsters, the source of "lobster tail," and the yearly catch outweighs that of the American lobster.

Crayfish belong to the family Astacidae which comes from the Greek word meaning "lobster or crayfish." Rich Romans fattened these lobster-like freshwater crustaceans in pools while slaves ate stream-caught varieties. Ever since, gourmets have dined on crayfish reared in ponds all over Europe and the southeastern United States. Economically important, over 8,280,000 pounds of crayfish were collected in the United States in 1976 alone, to be used as food and for study in biology classrooms.

More than 500 species are known, most less than six inches in length. They are found under rocks or debris in all types of shallow, freshwater environments throughout the world. Many burrow up to 10 feet or more, through dry ground, to find the water table. In marshy areas of Mississippi and Alabama, crayfish construct more than 30,000 burrows per acre, and can damage good crop land. Chimney-like mounds of earth may mark the location of a colony of these crayfish on a seemingly dry prairie. Their burrows are flooded with the water necessary for these animals to keep their gills wet in order to breathe. Dozens of crayfish species have adapted to life in pitch black caves, losing, in the process, their colors as well as their eyes.

Crayfish, regionally called crawfish, crawdads or crabs, walk on stout legs, but often quickly flap their tails to swim backwards at surprising speeds.

All species carry a pair of stout pincers for crushing or tearing food and for defense. Crayfish are scavengers and eat anything, but aquatic vegetation makes up the bulk of their diet. In many freshwater exhibits, especially in Gallery 4, the secretive, nocturnal crayfish clean up any food left uneaten by other species.

Crabs

Every crab brandishes a pair of clawed front legs. Hermit crabs and their relatives live in empty snail shells, but will even hide their soft abdomens in cartridge cases and tin cans. When disturbed, a hermit crab may completely withdraw into its shell house, sealing the entryway with its large claw. Carrying their adopted homes wherever they go, hermit crabs are found throughout the world in cold, warm and tropical seas. Some spend much of their lives on land, but always near water. Most species are small, except for the giant hermit, *Petrochirus diogenes,* of the Caribbean, that weighs more than a pound, and totes a huge conch or whelk shell on its back.

Spiny mithrax crab
Mithrax spinosissimus

Sponge crabs, *Dromia,* find protection by hollowing out the underside of a live sponge and holding it firmly on their backs with modified hind legs. Both the perfectly camouflaged crabs and sponges thrive with this arrangement. These crabs are found throughout the Caribbean Sea.

The well-named flame box crab, *Calappa,* is also known as the shame-faced crab because of its habit of holding very large forearms and claws in front of its face. This bottom-dweller escapes detection by partially burrowing in the sand.

Swimming crabs, such as the edible blue crab, *Callinectes sapidus,* use flattened hind legs as paddles to actively, if clumsily, swim. Their large front pincers pick and tear apart food. They occur throughout temperate and tropical seas. A few coastal species, including the commercially valuable blue crab, may enter the mouths of rivers and live entirely in fresh water for a time. Molting soft-shelled blue crabs bring high prices in sea food markets.

The mud crabs include the valuable stone crab, *Menippe mercenaria,* common in shallow oceans. Crabbers remove only one claw, as allowed by law. If both were removed, the crab would be defenseless and unable to gather food. The lost claw is usually restored after several molts.

Other commercially important crabs include the cancer crabs named after the crab-shaped star constellation. These heavy-bodied crabs wield strong arms and claws, and the hindmost pair of legs is adapted for running. The coldwater Dungeness crab of the northwest coast of North America, prized among crabs for its flavor, grows to more than seven inches across the oval-shaped body.

The spider crabs walk on long legs, and many sport large claws. The arrow crab of the Caribbean, *Stenorhynchus seticornis,* the most spider-like of the group, has an inch-long body, dwarfed by nine-inch-long legs that end in narrow claws. Decorator crabs, also in this family, camouflage their backs and legs with pieces of algae, sponge or hydroids. Other decorator crabs become the color of their immediate habitat, such as the green of an algae bed, or the red of a sponge colony, after eating a little of their surroundings.

Land-dwelling crabs include the red mangrove or tree crabs, *Goniopsis cruentata,* from Florida and the fiddler crabs, *Uca pugilator,* abundant on the east coast. Only the male fiddler carries the mismatched claws for which it is named. The large claw is the bow, which the crab sweeps back and forth across the smaller "fiddle."

Blue swimming crab
Callinectes sapidus

Hermit crab, *Dardanus* sp., carrying anemones.

Anemone porcelain crab
Petrolisthes maculatus

serpent stars
subclass **Ophiuroidea**

starfish
basket stars
subclass **Asteroidea**

sea lilies
class **Crinoidea**

sea urchins
sand dollars
class **Echinoidea**

sea cucumbers
class **Holothuroidea**

Spiny-skinned Animals

phylum Echinodermata

Sea lilies, starfish, serpent stars, sea urchins and sand dollars are among the 6,000 kinds of echinoderms found in all shallow oceans. Their name means "spiny skin," referring to bony plates barely covered by a thin skin. Tube feet, operated by a complex hydraulic system, slowly but surely carry starfish, sea urchins and sand dollars along the bottom. Rows of feet that end in suction discs firmly grip rocks when heavy currents or tides threaten to pull the animal loose. Starfish use the inexhaustible energy of many tube feet to pull apart the two halves of an oyster shell.

Sea Lilies
Most sea lilies, or crinoids, rhythmically wave up to two hundred arms when swimming through the sea. At rest, the sea lily holds onto objects with a few specialized graspers. The largest species gather food in feathery arms over 27 inches long. Deepwater, stalked forms are little changed from ancestors that flourished millions of years ago. Crinoids are seldom exhibited.

Starfish
Starfish, often called sea stars, range in size from less than an inch to more than three feet across. Most have five arms, or multiples of five, such as the forty-armed sun star, *Heliaster,* of the west coast of North America.

Some sea stars, especially the deep-sea species, feed on whatever is available. The scavenging, shallow-water

Many tube feet line the underside of a starfish.

bat star, *Patiria miniata,* everts its stomach over a rock to digest its cover of algae. The common star, *Asterias,* of the northeastern United States, feeds on clams and oysters. After pulling the shells apart, it inserts its own thin-walled stomach and digests the shellfish on the spot. In the past, oystermen used to slice up the hated starfish caught eating their livelihood, until they learned about its remarkable ability to grow back lost parts. A starfish cut into five equal pieces could, in time, grow into five separate starfish.

The intricate basket star, *Gorgonocephalus,* grows to over 36 inches across, its five arms branching and weaving a basket-like network that filters plankton at night. By day, the basket starfish forms a compact ball, wrapping itself tightly around an object, a sea fan, for example.

Chocolate chip starfish
Protoriaster nodosus

Serpent Stars
The serpent stars rely on the sinuous, serpentine pull of their arms to move along the bottom faster than any other echinoderm. Often called brittle stars, they readily cast off a leg from the distinct central disc when alarmed

Red crinoid

Basket star at night, arms extended.

Brittle star

or handled, but like all sea stars, will grow a new one. Serpent stars feed at night by scavenging, sifting bottom sediments for the associated plants and animals or by trapping plankton on mucus-lined arms that are waved through the water.

Sea Urchins and Sand Dollars

These armless relatives of starfish walk slowly about the ocean floor on tube feet. Sea urchins resemble pin cushions armed with spines of varying shapes. The club-spined urchin, *Eucidaris,* is sparsely covered by thickened, blunt spines which discourage predators' attempts to swallow it. They also help wedge the urchin into crevices, holding it secure even in heavy surf zones. *Diadema,* the long-spined urchin, bristles with densely packed, long, pointed, brittle spines. The short blunt spines of the green sea urchin, *Lytechinus,* offer it only moderate protection from predators, so this urchin camouflages itself with bits of broken shell and plants. Others, such as *Echinometra,* the rock-boring urchin, wedge into small depressions in coral rock with their spines, then enlarge the hiding place by wearing away the rock with the spines and chewing action of the mouth. Most sea urchins graze on vegetation or bottom material.

Flat, circular sand dollars, *Encope,* look fuzzy when alive, covered by many fine, velvety spines. They usually burrow slightly into the bottom, which they sift for tiny pieces of food. Some species filter plankton from the water.

Live sand dollar
Echinarachnius parma

Baja sand dollar skeleton.
Encope grandis

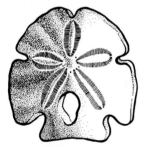

Long-spined sea urchins
Diadema

Tricolor sea cucumber, or sea apple,
Paracucumaria tricolor

Sea Cucumbers

Sea cucumbers have no spines for defense. When threatened, some species expel their internal organs, the oozy mess discouraging would-be-predators. Many are long and sausage-shaped, while others, known as sea apples, are plump and round. A circlet of tentacles surrounding a sea cucumber's mouth is used by some to sift sediments as they burrow along the bottom.

The tricolor sea cucumber, *Paracucumaria tricolor,* filters small animals from the water with its many branching arms. Other species pick up bits of food in mucus-covered tentacles as they crawl across the sandy sea floor. Some scoop up mouthfuls of sand, digesting any edible parts.

Sea cucumbers range in size from three inches to more than three feet, and inhabit cool to warm marine waters throughout the world.

Golden sea cucumber

Sea squirts

Sea Squirts

phylum Chordata

Sea squirts are small but common inhabitants of all types of marine environments. They are sedentary and may be solitary or colonial. Sea squirts live attached to wharves, rocks, sea grasses and mangroves. Some grow to more than seven inches in height. Their simple-looking, sac-like shape disguises the complex structures inside. The fact that the young possess a supporting backbone-like rod, called the notochord, makes them one of the most advanced of all the invertebrates.

Sea squirts are filter feeders, pumping water into their sac-like tunics through one opening, across a strainer and out through the other opening. When handled, the sea squirt shoots water from one of its two pores.

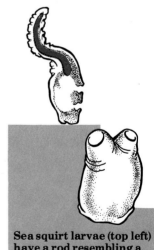

Sea squirt larvae (top left) have a rod resembling a backbone, which disappears in adulthood. Adults (above) resemble sponges but have two openings.

Fishes

Maroon anemonefish
Premnas biaculeatus

Hagfishes

family Myxinidae   order Myxiniformes

Slimy-bodied "hags" are strictly ocean fishes, abundant along Atlantic and Pacific coasts in water colder than 55°F. Their slender bodies end in distinctive, jawless sucker mouths. Wriggling into mouths or boring through the body wall of larger fishes, such as flounders, haddock and lingcod, they eat their hosts from the inside out, to the dismay of commercial fishermen. They also scavenge food on the sea floor.

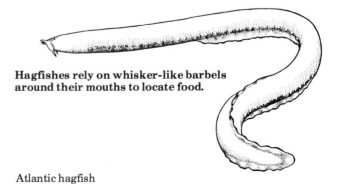

Hagfishes rely on whisker-like barbels around their mouths to locate food.

Atlantic hagfish
Myxine glutinosa

Lampreys

family Petromyzontidae   order Petromyzontiformes

Eel-like lampreys live in oceans and rivers and in the Great Lakes. They migrated from the Atlantic Ocean, up the St. Lawrence and into the lakes.

When man-made canals removed natural barriers, the parasitic sea lamprey, *Petromyzon marinus,* moved in and nearly wiped out native lake populations of lake trout, whitefish and ciscos. This in turn destroyed valuable commercial and sport fisheries. Smaller numbers of native chestnut lampreys, *Ichthyomyzon castaneus,* and silver lampreys, *Ichthyomyzon unicuspis,* were never a serious threat to fisheries.

Adult lampreys clamp onto a fish with their sucker mouths, gnaw a hole through the skin and feed, vampire-like, on its body fluids. After several days they drop off to find a fresh host. The weakened fish may die from the attack or more likely from secondary infections.

Non-parasitic species, brook lampreys, spend most of their lives as mud-dwelling larvae, where they filter plant and animal life from the water.

All lampreys ascend streams in the spring to spawn, where they build nests of stones, lay eggs and die. Larvae hatch 2–4 weeks later, drift downstream and live as filter feeders for 3–14 years, buried in muddy bottoms. Regular doses of lampricides poured into spawning streams have most effectively reduced the number of lampreys in the lakes.

Europeans commercially fish for brook lampreys, considered a delicacy, and King Henry I of England allegedly died from eating them in excess. Smoked lampreys are popular in Japan. In the United States, lamprey larvae are only considered good for bait.

Adults range in size from the 10-inch brook lamprey to larger, parasitic species that may reach three feet. Two dozen species are found in North America, Europe and Asia, from arctic to subantarctic regions.

The jawless lamprey has a sucker mouth with rows of sharp teeth that pierce and firmly grip larger fish. The scientific name, *Ichthyo-myzon,* means "sucking fish."

Silver lamprey
Ichthyomyzon unicuspis

Unlike true bony fishes, lampreys lack jaws, bones scales and paired fins.

Sharks

"Restless rovers of the seas," this great group of fishes is widely distributed throughout the oceans of the world, and even freshwater lakes and rivers. Most occur, however, in shallower waters of tropical and subtropical seas.

Sharks are among the earth's oldest living creatures. The first sharks swam in the oceans over 300 million years ago and were not that different from the more than 350 species known today. Sharks differ from true fishes by having lighter, more elastic skeletons made of cartilage, instead of bone. They also lack gas-filled swim bladders for buoyancy, making it necessary for them to swim continuously to avoid sinking.

Sharks vary in shape and swimming speed, from the sleek, high-speed thresher and mako sharks of the open sea to the heavier-set nurse and horn sharks that doze on the sea bottom.

Sharks feed on most other fish and marine life, including their own young. Despite their reputation as man-eaters, only 30 or so shark species are potentially harmful to man. Several of these belong to the family Lamnidae that includes the great white and mako sharks. (A mythical Greek monster, Lamia, was a "horrible man-eating creature" and possible source of the scientific name.) The bizarre hammerhead shark, family Sphyrnidae, is also notorious for its aggressiveness towards people.

Sharks range in size from the plankton-eating, 65-foot whale shark, *Rhincodon typus,* the largest of all fish, to the six-inch dwarf shark, *Squaliolus laticaudus.* Regardless of size, all sharks have cartilaginous

Great white shark
Carcharodon carcharias

skeletons, five to seven gill slits, and many rows of teeth anchored in strong, tissue-covered jaws. Sharks replace frequently lost teeth from these reserves; some species produce thousands of teeth in a lifetime.

Almost all sharks are carnivorous, possessing either narrow and pointed or triangular and serrated teeth for biting and seizing prey. Others have flattened molars for crushing shellfish. The two largest species, whale and basking sharks, strain plankton and small fish from the ocean, their huge mouths containing only small teeth amidst the gill rakers and whisker-like baleen.

Whatever they eat, sharks usually hear their prey first, hundreds of yards away, before they smell it or see it. Their lateral lines pick up vibrations and pressure waves caused by objects disturbing the water several hundred feet away. Sharks also use their unique system of sensory cells, called "ampullae of Lorenzini," to decipher the surrounding waters. Through these nerve endings in the skin around the head region, a shark receives information about salinity, pressure, temperature and, most importantly, electrical current. They have the highest sensitivity to electrical fields of any animal. Sharks, rays and skates use this to detect the tiny electrical signals given off by all animals, a camouflaged flounder buried in the sea floor, for example. Migratory sharks may also orient themselves in the open sea using the earth's magnetic field.

Imbedded in the thick hide of every shark are hundreds of small, tooth-like denticles (denticle means "little tooth"). In some regions of the world, dried shark skin serves as sandpaper. A tough, high-quality leather is made from the skins of larger sharks for use in handbags, shoes, wallets, watch straps and belts.

Man, in fact, rivals the natural predators of sharks — killer whales and other sharks — and has greatly reduced the numbers of certain species through commercial and sport fisheries, incidental killings by fishermen and in barrier nets designed to protect swimming beaches.

Commercially, shark meat is popular in Europe and Asia and has become more acceptable in the United States, where it is often marketed under different names, such as greyfish. In England, millions of pounds of dogfish are consumed each year in the form of the popular "fish and chips." Sharkfin soup is a favorite in China and Japan, where many species are also served smoked and fresh. Before synthetic vitamin production, oily shark livers, rich in vitamin A, were prized. Small quantities of shark oil are still used in tanning leather, in barometers and as lubricants. Squalene, a component of shark oil, goes into cosmetics and pharmaceuticals in Japan.

Sharks either lay eggs or bear live young, depending on the species. The live-born young hatch from eggs within the mother's body and at birth fully resemble adults. Others litter the ocean floor with leathery, keratin egg cases in a variety of distinctive shapes and sizes, each protecting an individual embryo and its nourishing yolk sac.

Many of the larger, nomadic shark species do not take kindly to captivity. The great white shark, *Carcharodon carcharias,* known as "white death" in Australia, has never been kept successfully in aquariums despite continuing research and ongoing attempts to do so. Little is known about this efficient predator, which may reach lengths greater than 21 feet. It is one of the sharks that must swim continuously to keep oxygen-rich water moving over its gills, and so requires vast amounts of space. Its extreme sensitivity to the electrical properties of metal, an element present in most exhibit tanks, further hampers display efforts.

Great whites eat everything from squid to sea mammals, including whales. While easily capable of devouring people, the documented records of "bite and release" attacks may disprove the great white's evil reputation. Scientists believe that those attacks may be cases of mistaken identity, the shark immediately spitting out the person it had mistaken for a seal, or other marine mammal. Sources agree that of the 50 or so shark attacks reported annually (only about 10 of these are fatal), not all can be attributed to great whites. Other "man-eaters" include bull sharks and hammerheads.

Many of the quieter, inshore species of sharks thrive in captivity. From time to time, the Aquarium expects to exhibit representatives of most of the following families.

Horn shark
Heterodontus francisci

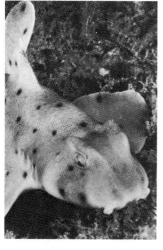

Horn or Bullhead Sharks

family Heterodontidae   order Heterodontiformes

Small and harmless, bullhead or horn sharks occur in the shallows of the Indo-Pacific but not in the Atlantic or Mediterranean. The name bullhead and the less commonly used "pighead" describe the knobby, oversized appearance of their heads.

All of the sharks in this family have mouths adapted for feeding on bottom-dwelling clams and shellfish. Their sharp front teeth are pointed for biting and seizing, while molars in back crush hard shells, hence the name Heterodontidae, which means "different teeth."

Horn sharks lay eggs, tucking them into rock crevices where the leathery cases harden and are difficult to remove. These unusually shaped egg cases, occasionally seen on exhibit during efforts to hatch the young, are large, brown, elongated capsules adorned with a double spiral flange.

The horn shark, *Heterodontus francisci,* from the coast of California, lives up to its common name by sporting a stout spine in front of each of its two dorsal fins. Buff or brown, this little shark grows to four feet in length.

Horn shark egg case

Nurse Sharks

Nurse shark
Ginglymostoma cirratum

family Orectolobidae   order Squaliformes

Unlike open ocean sharks, nurse sharks can lie for hours on shallow, sunlit ocean floors. They actively pump water over their gills, eliminating the need to swim constantly in order to breathe. Groups may pile up in two to ten feet of water under ledges, in caves, near reefs or in turtle grass beds.

At night, nurse sharks forage for meals, sucking in crabs, lobsters and sea urchins which they crush with powerful jaws. Whisker-like barbels near their small mouths feel or taste for food along the bottom, detecting animals hidden in the sand. Like all sharks, they also have acute senses of hearing and smell.

Nurse sharks will attack when provoked, and since they share shallow, murky waters with bathers and divers, this occurs with some frequency. They may mistake feet and legs for food.

Their rough skin is the most valued in the "shagreen" or leather industry.

Nurse sharks bear live young, but the common name does not refer to any known nurturing behavior. It may have derived from a Middle English word for a type of shark, "huss;" a "huss" shark becoming a nurse shark.

An Australian form, the wobbegong, has a color pattern reminiscent of an old-fashioned carpet, giving rise to another common family name, carpet shark.

The Atlantic nurse shark, *Ginglymostoma cirratum,* is the only one of the two dozen species of nurse sharks that occurs in the Atlantic, ranging from North Carolina to the West Indies, Brazil and along the west coast of Africa. All others are common in the Indo-Pacific. They reach a length of 14 feet and do well in captivity, one having lived at the Aquarium for 25 years.

Cat Sharks
family Scyliorhinidae   order Squaliformes

These are small, harmless, often deepwater sharks known throughout the Pacific, especially near Australia, South Africa and the coast of California. Atlantic species known as dogfishes (not to be confused with the true dogfishes, Squalidae), are a nuisance to commercial fishermen who pull them up in great numbers in their nets.

One member of the family, the swell shark, *Cephaloscyllium ventriosum,* frequents the kelp beds of the California coast, where at night it prowls the ocean floor for shellfish. When frightened, swell sharks inflate their stomachs with air or water, perhaps to wedge themselves into a hiding place or to appear larger to predators. These small, quiet sharks reach lengths of about three feet.

Requiem Sharks
family Carcharhinidae   order Squaliformes

Truly shark-like in their appearance, members of this largest family of sharks are common throughout the world's seas. Many species are aggressive, including the feared tiger, oceanic whitetip and the bull shark, *Carcharhinus leucas.*

The bull shark even ventures into brackish and fresh water, entering some lakes and rivers in South America, Australia, Africa, India and North America. The

Mississippi Delta region may be a spawning ground, and bull sharks have been sighted in the Mississippi River as far north as Alton, Illinois. A notoriously aggressive species, the bull shark "bites people more frequently than any other species" according to one source, and fatal attacks are well documented.

The lemon shark, *Negaprion brevirostris,* thrives in captivity and often appears in aquariums, making it perhaps the best known of the requiems. Star of many early shark studies, it has the reputation of being a quick learner. These medium-size, yellow-backed sharks can be distinguished by two dorsal fins of the same size; other requiems have a larger one in front.

Lemon sharks live near bays, sounds and river mouths along the Atlantic coast from New Jersey to northern Brazil, and are common around the Florida Keys. They reach lengths of 11 feet and can be dangerous, attacking without provocation.

One of the most vividly marked requiem sharks also thrives in aquariums worldwide because of its remarkable ability to tolerate shipping without serious ill effects. The leopard shark, *Triakis semifasciata,* blends into its native kelp forest habitat along the Pacific coast from Oregon to southern California. This harmless, quiet species reaches a length of only five and one-half feet.

Leopard shark
Triakis semifasciata

Hammerhead Sharks

family Sphyrnidae   order Squaliformes

Ernest Hemingway described an attacking hammerhead shark's bizarre appearance: the "yard-wide mouth... the great horns of its head with the eyes on the end, spread wide," in *Islands in the Stream*. This group of sharks is notorious for its ferocity and is often first on the scene in baited waters. Its reputation as a man-eater is well documented.

In schools or swimming alone, hammerheads occur in all tropical seas, venturing into temperate waters only in the summer. The largest species reach lengths of 20 feet, with heads three feet wide. Rarely seen in aquariums, they are "fragile" and do not survive in captivity.

Oppian, the Roman poet, is said to have called these sharks "the balance fish" because of their strangely shaped heads. Scientists speculate that the "hammer" heads aid these predators in finding prey, and give them increased maneuverability. The front edge of the wide head is peppered with sensory pits, which detect chemical, physical, thermal and electrical changes in water. One source likens the shark to a minesweeper — the fish sweeping its head over the ocean floor to detect a favorite prey, stingrays, buried in the sand.

One quieter, harmless species, the bonnethead, *Sphyrna tiburo,* lives well in captivity. It is easily captured in the shallow coastal waters of the Atlantic from New England to Brazil. Smallest of the hammerheads, it rarely exceeds five feet. Its shovel-like, rounded head is less dramatic than that of its larger cousin.

Sawfishes

family Pristidae   order Rajiformes

A sawfish bears a long "double-edged sword" that reaches six feet in the largest species, and measures a foot wide at the base. These fish may exceed 25 feet in length, although the average is 15–20 feet. Slashing rapidly through a school of fish, sawfish wield their hefty snouts like a sword, killing and wounding prey with the sword's stout teeth. They then cruise back through the wounded fish, sucking up the dead and dying victims. Often, sawfish stir up the sea floor in search of invertebrates and other bottom-dwelling animals.

The sword is lined with sharp teeth of the same size, varying in number between 17 to 32 pairs, depending on the species. At birth, teeth are soft and covered by tissue to protect the mother, hardening on contact with sea water. Sawfish teeth have been found imbedded in undersea cables, an indication of their bottom-feeding behavior.

Sawfishes are considered a nuisance fish because they slash and tear the nets and trawls of fishermen. The three species are common throughout the shallow waters of all tropical seas, and are known to occur in estuaries and fresh water. The largest species, the greater small-toothed sawfish, *Pristis pectinata,* lives well in captivity and can quickly outgrow even the 90,000-gallon Coral Reef Exhibit. Despite its size, it is usually docile and can be fed by hand.

Smalltoothed sawfish
Pristis pectinata

Atlantic electric ray
Torpedo nobiliana

The wide pectoral fins of an
electric, or torpedo, ray
contain electric organs,
which are used to stun prey.

Electric Rays

family Torpedinidae   order Rajiformes

The electrical discharges given off by the rays in this
family have been known throughout history, appearing
in the writings of early Greeks. Romans used an electric
ray shock treatment as a cure for gout, headache and
mental illness. The majority of torpedo rays produce
75–80 volts, but the largest species may send out a
powerful discharge of 200 volts, strong enough to stun a
person.

A ray uses its electrical output for protection and to
capture food. Small fish are enveloped within the ray's
wide pectoral fins, which contain the electrical organs.
Its discharge either kills or stuns the prey that it could
not otherwise catch with its small mouth.

Electric rays inhabit all tropical, subtropical and
temperate seas, from the shallows to 3,000 feet. They lie
concealed in sand, partially buried, and further hidden
by their coloration. The largest species, the Atlantic
electric ray, *Torpedo nobiliana,* may exceed five feet in
length. Torpedo rays do not have tail spines.

Skates

family Rajidae   order Rajiformes

Skates resemble their close relatives, the rays, in
appearance and behavior. Their names are incorrectly
used interchangeably. Both are flat, bottom-dwelling
fishes,which glide and soar through the water on greatly
enlarged pectoral fins. Skates, however, have noticeably
larger eyes and tails shorter than their bodies. They
never have venomous tail spines. Skates lay eggs, while
rays give birth to live young. Some of the more than 100
species of skate generate weak electrical impulses, but
they do so with organs in the tail, not in the wings like
the more powerful electric rays.

Skates are widely distributed throughout the
temperate and cold oceans, and in deeper water in the
tropics. European fishermen trawl for the valued wing
meat of the roker, or thornback ray, *Raja clavata,* a true
skate despite its name. In shallow American waters
from Novia Scotia to North Carolina, the winter skate,
Raja ocellata, preys heavily on valuable commercial
species of shellfish, crabs and shrimps, invoking the
wrath of fishermen. Skate meat tastes similar to more
expensive scallops, but can be distinguished by the
direction of the grain.

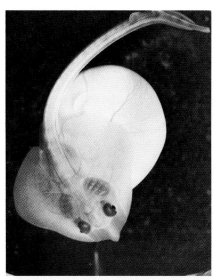

Clearnose skate embryo
Raja eglanteria

Roundel skate
Raja texana

"Mermaid's purses," or skate egg cases, wash on shore where beach combers or predatory birds may find the tough, leathery, oblong shelters that each house an immature skate attached to its yolk sac. Curled tendrils at the corners normally anchor clumps of egg cases to objects on the bottom. The large, long-snouted skate of the Pacific, *Raja binoculata,*which grows to eight feet, produces foot-long egg cases. From time to time, clearnose skate embryos will be removed from their keratin cases and placed on display in small tanks.

Skate egg cases

Stingrays

family Dasyatidae   order Rajiformes

Stingrays are feared throughout their range because of their venom-laden tail spine. The thin tail, longer than the ray's body, flexes in all directions and with enough force to imbed the spine in bone or wood. The ray will replace the lost spine and usually carries a spare. The painful wounds inflicted by these shallow-water rays may be fatal if a person is injured in the chest or stomach. Rays are difficult to see because they lie half-buried in the sand in the shallows of all oceans. The Pacific stingray, *Dasyatis brevicaudata,* may reach a hefty 750 pounds, with a 7-foot wing span and 14-foot length. Its 16-inch tail spine is a dangerous weapon. The smaller species only attain a disc width of 12 inches.

Rays flap their pectoral fins in the sand to uncover clams and bivalves, grinding them with strong, numerous crushing teeth. Fishermen dislike them for the

Blue-spotted stingray
Taeniura lymma

Cownose rays
Rhinoptera bonasus

devastation they cause to commercially valuable shellfish beds and the threat they pose when incidentally caught in trawls.

In the Indo-Pacific, cleaned stingray spines serve as weapons, either as a single spear tip or tied together in bundles. In parts of Africa, whips are made from the flexible tails, and the skins reverberate as drumheads.

The southern stingray, *Dasyatis americana,* is the most common of the Atlantic and Caribbean species, and may exceed five feet in length.

River Stingrays
family Potamotrygonidae   order Rajiformes

Freshwater stingrays, like their marine cousins, are abundant in shallow bottom areas and are also feared by fishermen because of the painful injuries they inflict. A pointed, serrated spine growing on the base of the tail carries a venom that attacks the nervous system and heart, and occasionally causes death.

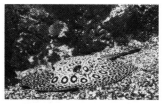

Ocellated freshwater stingray
Potamotrygon motoro

River stingrays, *Potamotrygon,* are small, usually less than two feet in diameter. They conceal their circular, spotted bodies in the mud or sand of rivers in central and northern South America and West Africa.

Like all rays and skates, they use unique electro-sensors to detect the weak electrical signals given off by other animals sharing their murky river habitat.

Eagle Rays, Cownose Rays
family Myliobatidae   order Rajiformes

Soaring and gliding through tropical and temperate seas on widespread pectoral-fin "wings," eagle rays equal their namesakes in swiftness and grace. They are notorious jumpers, bursting from the surface for reasons that remain unclear. Though fast swimmers, these active rays feed on the bottom, crushing the toughest of clam shells and invertebrates. They could destroy commercial clam and oyster beds if not kept out by close-set poles.

This family includes the cownose rays, named for the fleshy, divided upper and lower "lips," a family characteristic carried to an extreme.

Schools of 4,000 to 6,000 cownose rays, *Rhinoptera bonasus,* migrate along the Atlantic coast from New England to Brazil. This species reaches a length of two feet; other cownose rays may measure seven feet tip to tip.

Lungfishes

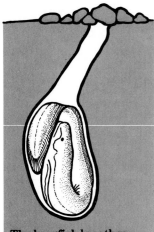

The lungfish breathes through small air holes in its cocoon, and lives off its muscle tissue, losing up to half its weight.

As the world's waters receded about 300 million years ago, lungfishes survived in drying or stagnant pools by breathing air. They are one of the few types of fishes with true lungs.

The three families of these ancient fishes inhabit regions that seasonally experience periods of drought. The Australian species, unlike the others, prefers shallow pools and backwaters that never dry up. It survives in weedy lagoons by gulping air every 30 to 60 minutes into its single lung, and can live totally submerged.

The African and South American lungfishes, however, drown if unable to come to the surface to take air into their pair of lungs. When their tropical freshwater pools dry up between rainy seasons, these lungfish, or "mud-sirens," survive by burrowing into mud tunnels, within waterproof cocoons. The annual rains bring them out of their dormant period. Lungfishes were once considered as the possible links between the fishes and the amphibians because these fishes breathe air and a few "stand" on leg-like fins.

An Australian lungfish, *Neoceratodus forsteri,* holds an unusual longevity record at the Aquarium, having been on exhibit since 1933.

Australian Lungfish

family Ceratodidae   order Ceratodiformes

The large, heavily scaled Australian lungfish, *Neoceratodus forsteri,* does not burrow or tunnel in the mud during dry seasons like the other species. A lethargic animal, it feeds on bottom-dwellers, slow-moving fish or plants. A once-valued food fish, it is now protected by international treaty.

South American Lungfish

family Lepidosirenidae   order Lepidosireniformes

The single species, *Lepidosiren paradoxa,* is abundant in densely weeded swamps and streams in central South America. Females lay thousands of eggs in nests guarded by the males. Young fish have external gills that later disappear, and in this respect are similar to the African species.

South American lungfish
Lepidosiren paradoxa

Shortfin bichir
Polypterus palmas

African Lungfishes

family Protopteridae   order Lepidosireniformes

The four African species of lungfish are very similar in appearance and behavior to the South American family. They are valued as food within their range, easily dug up in their mud-ball cocoons, caught in nets or speared.

Young lungfish are popular aquarium fish. The most popular species, *Protopterus annectens,* rarely exceeds two feet, while adult *Protopterus aethiopicus* may measure five feet or more.

Bichirs

family Polypteridae   order Polypteriformes

In the densely weeded shallows of African lakes and rivers, long, slender fishes prowl the bottom for small frogs and fishes. Occasionally surfacing, bichirs and reedfishes breathe air through lung-like organs in order to survive in these stagnant, tropical waters. They can live for several days out of water.

Many "finlets" run like a row of little flags along the bichir's back, earning the family name Polypteridae, which means "many fins."

Most bichirs are drab except for the popular, foot-long aquarium species *Polypterus delhezi* and *Polypterus ornatipinnis,* and the more beautiful, snake-like reedfish, *Calamoichthys calabaricus.*

Shovelnose sturgeon
Scaphirhynchus platorynchus

Sturgeons

family Acipenseridae   order Acipenseriformes

Legendary in its size, the largest sturgeon of all is the giant beluga, *Huso huso,* setting a record at 28 feet and 2,860 pounds.

Ponderous fishes reaching massive proportions, sturgeons take more than 20 years to reach maturity, and may live for more than 150 years. These sluggish, armor-plated fishes drag their barbels along sandy or gravelly bottoms, straining small animals from the material sucked into their underslung mouths.

Sturgeons occur only in the northern hemisphere, in cool lakes, rivers or oceans, and all ascend rivers to spawn. Their eggs, or roe, command a high price when salted and sold as caviar. Further demand for the flesh and once-valuable air bladders (source of isinglass, used as a gelatin and to clarify wine) have contributed to the decline of nearly all species of these slow-growing fishes. Pollution of lake habitats and damming of spawning streams caused further decline.

Lake sturgeon, *Acipenser fulvescens,* were once considered trash fish in their midwest range. During the 1800s, a short-lived commercial fishery rapidly depleted the stock of up to 100-pound sturgeon. Today, only a small Lake Michigan population exists. Sturgeon are occasionally caught in the Mississippi River and are fished or speared through the ice in Lake Winnebago, Wisconsin. Two, six-foot lake sturgeon lived for over 43 years at the Aquarium.

The smaller, three-foot shovelnose sturgeon, *Scaphirhynchus platorynchus,* meaning "spade snout, broad snout," still thrives in the Mississippi Valley.

Largest of all the freshwater fish in North America, the huge white sturgeon, *Acipenser transmontanus,* from the Pacific Coast, now averages only 300 pounds. Undocumented records describe an 1,800 pound female and other specimens over 15 feet.

Heavily fished, the giant beluga, *Huso huso,* is being raised by Russian aquaculturists attempting to increase populations in the Caspian and Black Seas, and Volga River. In 1971, the Aquarium received small beluga sturgeons as a result of a special exchange between the United States and Russia.

The Atlantic sturgeon, *Acipenser oxyrhynchus,* also declining in numbers, lives in the ocean and ascends rivers on both shores of the Atlantic to spawn.

Juvenile paddlefish
Polyodon spathula

Paddlefishes

family Polyodontidae   order Acipenseriformes

Paddlefish, *Polyodon spathula,* live and feed near the surface of deep pools and large rivers. Opening their wide mouths located beneath broad snouts, these fish sweep their heads slightly from side to side. Swimming constantly, they strain plankton from huge volumes of water.

The distinctive snout is covered with sensors that orient these fish in their murky river habitat and help in locating concentrations of food.

Early explorers of the Mississippi River system wrote of huge, curious-looking paddlefish weighing hundreds of pounds. Today, this species averages 60 pounds and three and one-half feet in length in its greatly reduced range east of the Rocky Mountains. Habitat destruction has reduced natural populations, as did overfishing.

Today, sport fishermen snag paddlefish in man-made lakes near dams, where they occasionally occur in substantial numbers.

The two living species remaining in this family of primitive fishes occur in widely separated areas: *Polyodon spathula* in North America and the larger *Psephurus gladius,* limited to the Yangtze River in China.

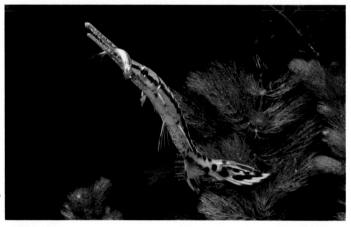

Juvenile longnose gar, *Lepisosteus osseus,* eating a minnow.

Gars

family Lepisosteidae   order Semionotiformes

Warm rivers and lakes in much of North America and Mexico conceal gars hanging motionless in shallow, weedy areas.

To other fish, gars may resemble harmless logs drifting near the surface, until a sudden lunge rewards the gar with a meal.

Efficient and important predators, they control fish populations but earn the disfavor of competing fishermen. Their strong jaws and sharp teeth destroy nets and gear. Gars have the unenviable reputation of being nuisances and "thieves" and themselves are rarely valued as food.

All gars are in the single genus *Lepisosteus,* which means "bony scale." Longnose gars, *Lepisosteus osseus,* the most abundant species, are common from the Great Lakes region south to Florida and Mexico. Tenacious of life, they live over 20 years in captivity, reaching lengths of four to five feet.

Shortnose gars, *Lepisosteus platostomus* ("broad-mouth"), have shorter snouts. They also lack the dark spots of the similar, spotted gars, *Lepisosteus oculatus.* (The name means "provided with eyes" in reference to its many spots.) Both seldom grow larger than two and one-half feet long.

Alligator gars, *Lepisosteus spatula* ("spoon," referring to the broad snout), take after their reptilian namesake in size and feeding style. Among the largest of North American freshwater fishes, the 10-foot long, 300-pound record dwarfs the average length of six or seven feet. Common in salt or brackish water in southern states, the alligator gar also occurs in the Mississippi River system. Reportedly ferocious, it supplements its fish diet with ducks and other waterfowl. The gar's large, diamond-shaped scales supplied Indians with arrowheads and material for jewelry. A few regional commercial fisheries still exist.

Alligator gars live for a long time, and several were exhibited in the Aquarium for over 40 years.

Bowfin

family Amiidae   order Amiiformes

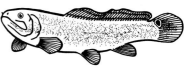

Bowfin
Amia calva

The bowfin, *Amia calva,* is the only species of this ancient order of fishes living today. Except for Lake Superior, it lives in all the Great Lakes and throughout the Mississippi River system.

A fish of many names — dogfish, mudfish, spotfin, choupique, cottonfish, poisson marais ("fish of the marshes"), lake lawyer and John A. Grindle — it is easily recognized. A single, long, rippling dorsal fin stretches to the tail, which is decorated with a brightly ringed dark spot.

Bowfins share gars' tenacity of life, and also their destructive reputation. They are hardy fish that survive low oxygen levels and can live out of water for many hours. Highly predatory, they gorge themselves on small fishes. When caught on hook and line, their fight equals or excels that of a northern pike or bass.

Mooneyes

family Hiodontidae   order Osteoglossiformes

The aptly named mooneyes hunt at night in cool lakes throughout the northern, central and eastern parts of the United States. Most members of the family are prized as game fish. Mooneye, *Hiodon tergisus,* is the only species of its family in the Great Lakes basin.

Goldeye, *Hiodon alosoides,* considered by some "the most flavorful fish in Canada," is served smoked in southern Canada.

Featherbacks

family Notopteridae   order Osteoglossiformes

One small "feathery" fin adorns the bare humpback of some species of featherbacks. On the underside, a long fin ripples from the head to the tip of the tail, propelling the fish easily backwards or forwards. Inactive by day, they linger near the surface under vegetation, feeding on small fish, insects or shrimps, and occasionally gulping air.

The ocellated featherback, *Notopterus chitala,* thrives in swamps and rivers throughout India, Asia and Australia. In Thailand it is a choice food fish, where it is cultured from eggs spawned in the wild.

The smaller, more docile, false featherback, *Xenomystus nigri,* from West African rivers, has no "feather" dorsal fin.

The ocellated featherback fry, *Notopterus chitala,* below, was the first of its kind spawned in a public aquarium. The parents laid the eggs in their exhibit at the Aquarium in 1979.

Arawana, Arapaima

family Osteoglossidae   order Osteoglossiformes

The mighty arapaima and the lithesome arawana belong to a family of freshwater fishes known for their bony tongues. (Osteoglossidae means "bony tongue.") Throughout their South American range, dried tongues are traded and used as raspers to break down seeds. Large, bony scales are another family characteristic, converted by Amazonians into jewelry and trade goods.

The arapaima, *Arapaima gigas,* may be the largest strictly freshwater fish known. Many publications report lengths of 15 feet, but there is no documented evidence of fish this long. Ten feet seems to be the maximum. A fish of this size would weigh 550 pounds, according to a length-weight ratio. Although it is now protected by international treaty, the arapaima is still

The *pirarucu* is named for
the red scales near its tail:
pira means fish; *urucu* is the
name of the bush bearing
flaming red seeds that are a
source of annato dye.

Arapaima *Arapaima gigas*

Arawana
Osteoglossum bicirrhosum

fished and hunted throughout its range in the Amazon
river basin. It has long been exploited for its scales,
tongue and tasty flesh.

Arapaimas, known as *pirarucu* in Brazil and *paiche* in
Peru, glide or drift near the surface, breathing air every
10 to 20 minutes. They feed on smaller fishes that are
swallowed or sucked in with a tremendous gulp.
Arapaimas are notoriously excitable and have a
tendency to jump clear of exhibit tanks when startled.
The young are difficult to raise, although the Aquarium
received an eight-inch-long arapaima in 1954 that grew
to over seven feet and 200 pounds, setting a longevity
record of 18 years.

Approximating the arapaima's range and shallow
river habitat, the smaller arawana, *Osteoglossum
bicirrhosum,* only reaches lengths of about three feet. Its

species name describes the distinctive two barbels decorating its chin. The arawana cruises gracefully near the surface, breathing air and capturing fallen insects, animals or small fish in its sharply upturned mouth. It may leap entirely out of the water to seize fish, or even small birds from overhanging branches, earning it a regional nickname, "water-monkey."

Thought to be a mouth brooder, the female may carry babies in a pouch-like fold between the lower jawbones.

Bow and arrow fishermen hunt arawanas in river shallows near shore. Beautiful aquarium fish, they appear irridescent in the sunlight, the long rippling fins tinged pale blue.

Other species of bony tongues live in Africa, Asia and Australia, a fact scientists use as evidence for the theory that the land masses were once joined.

Freshwater Butterflyfish

family Pantodontidae   order Osteoglossiformes

Freshwater butterflyfish
Pantodon buchholzi

In the still waters of lush, tropical West African rivers, freshwater butterflyfish quietly stand among the plants on long, slender fins, watching the surface for fallen or low-flying insects. Bursting into the air, they glide distances of six feet or more on large, lacy pectoral fins. The naturalist Buchholz reportedly first discovered this small fish by catching one in a butterfly net as it skimmed over the surface of a pond. The fish is named after him, *Pantodon buchholzi*.

Elephantnose Fish, Mormyrids

family Mormyridae   order Mormyriformes

Mormyrids and elephantnose fishes send out weak electrical pulses to navigate through murky African rivers and lakes as well as to find food and locate each other. Ancient Egyptians depicted elephantnose fishes in tomb murals and jewelry.

Some mormyrids probe in mud for worms and insects with the long, curved snouts that resemble the trunks of elephants. Other species have finger-like feelers on their chins.

Larger species, such as the three-foot-long Nile elephantnose, *Mormyrus kannume,* are commercially harvested for food. The small, docile Ubangi mormyrid, *Gnathonemus petersi,* is a popular aquarium fish, as is its larger relative, *Gnathonemus stanleyanus.*

Ubangi mormyrid
Gnathonemus petersi

**The small electric organs of
the mormyrid are located
near its tail.**

**The knifefish sends out
weak electrical discharges
using organs derived from
muscles.**

Gymnarchus knifefish
Gymnarchus niloticus

Nile Knifefish

family Gymnarchidae   order Mormyriformes

Near the naked tail of the freshwater knifefish are four
organs that continuously discharge electrical pulses.
The knifefish holds its narrow body rigid, even while
swimming, to maintain the electrical field that it relies
on for navigating, finding food and detecting friend or
foe in the silty, muddy Nile River or murky African
lakes. Only the long, wavy fin along its back ripples as it
moves gracefully backwards or forwards, or surfaces to
gulp air.

　　The single species, *Gymnarchus niloticus,* grows to a
length of five feet and is closely related to the other
electrical African fishes, the mormyrids, Mormyridae,
but not to the South American knifefishes, Gymnotidae.

See page 101,
Aquatic Life: Fishes

Herring, Alewife, Gizzard Shad

family Clupeidae   order Clupeiformes

School of Atlantic herring
Clupea harengus

Billions of these silvery fishes swarm the seas. Herrings, sardines and over a hundred other species in this family are among the most important fishes commercially, supporting fisheries throughout the world's temperate and tropical oceans. Historically, the abundant herrings have been crucial to the development and economies of many coastal countries. Marketed fresh, smoked, salted, pickled, cured, canned or ground into fish meal and fertilizer, the billions of dollars at stake have led to armed disputes over fishing rights in European waters. Menhaden, *Brevoortia tyrannus,* rates as one of the most important species to the United States east coast fisheries.

Fishes in the herring family lose scales easily, making it very difficult to transport them unharmed for display. However, locally available alewives and gizzard shad may be exhibited from time to time.

The shads are herring-like fishes that live in the oceans but enter fresh water to spawn. This includes the alewife. The Atlantic American shad, *Alosa sapidissima,* now also flourishes on the west coast and in North American rivers since its introduction early in the twentieth century. Huge schools feed in plankton-rich surface waters and support healthy fisheries, especially during spring migrations into rivers. It is one of the best food fish in the family. Shad roe is considered a delicacy.

The plankton-eating alewife, *Alosa pseudoharengus,* is common in the ocean along the east coast from Nova Scotia to North Carolina as well as in freshwater lakes. Great Lakes populations migrated up rivers when man-made canals removed natural barriers, and now are the most abundant fish in Lake Michigan. Their population

Alewife
Alosa pseudoharengus

explosion began in the early 1950s after sea lampreys wiped out larger fish that would have kept alewives in check. Lampreys are now controlled, and alewives are an important forage fish for restocked lake trout and salmon valuable to sport fisheries. Commercial harvest of these fish that were once considered a nuisance has fallen off because of the high PCB levels in their oily flesh. During the peak population explosions, die-offs due to starvation and stress fouled beaches and waterways with billions of alewives.

Gizzard shad, *Dorosoma cepedianum,* are herring-like fish with heavily muscled stomachs that extract worms and small animals from the mouthfuls of mud they eat in streams and rivers.

Tarpons
family Elopidae   order Elopiformes

Atlantic tarpon, *Megalops atlanticus,* are world-famous game fish that will fight and leap until exhausted. The large, shiny scales of the "silver king" are used ornamentally by islanders.

The record catch is an eight-foot, 350-pound specimen. Anglers seek the average four-footer as far north as Cape Cod in the summer, although it is most abundant in tropical seas. The smaller Pacific, or ox-eye tarpon, *Megalops cyprinoides,* from the Indian and Pacific Oceans, seldom exceeds three and one-half feet.

Atlantic tarpon
Megalops atlanticus

Tarpon hunt at night, catching shrimp, mullet and other surface-feeding fish in their large, upturned mouths. An ability to gulp air allows the young to survive in the shelter of stagnant estuaries, mangroves and lagoons, which are avoided by larger fish.

In 1935, Aquarium collectors caught several young Atlantic tarpon. The sole survivor swims in the Coral Reef Exhibit, breaking all longevity records.

Bonefish
family Albulidae   order Elopiformes

Bonefish, *Albula vulpes,* are tough fighters. They are sought by sport fishermen despite their small size of three feet or less. They occur worldwide in tropical seas and are common around Florida and the Bahamas. Bonefish, unlike tarpon, feed on the bottom on worms, clams, crabs and shrimp.

Freshwater Eels
family Anguillidae   order Anguilliformes

Adult freshwater eels migrate from rivers and streams to the sea to spawn. Some travel vast distances, slithering over land damp with rain or dew, if necessary. They breathe through their skins while out of the water.

At sea, they lay millions of eggs in deep water and then die. Tiny, transparent, ribbon-like larvae float as plankton with the currents. After one to three years, they reach the home waters of their parents and transform into elvers, or glass eels, only inches long.

The young eels swim up rivers to assume the nocturnal habits of adults, voraciously hunting or scavenging. Full-grown eels reportedly prey on fish, ducklings and small mammals.

The European eel, *Anguilla anguilla,* is prized for its flesh, whether marketed live or smoked. Fishermen net the migrating eels at river mouths as they set out for ocean spawning grounds. At this time, the fattened females measure four to six feet, while the adult males are only two feet long.

The American eel, *Anguilla rostrata,* receives less attention from east coast fishermen, although exports to Japan are increasing. This Atlantic species is common in harbors, estuaries, marshes and rivers as far inland as the midwest, and like the European species, also migrates to the Sargasso Sea to spawn.

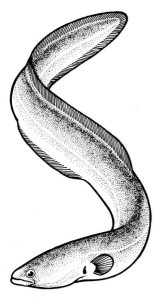

American eel
Anguilla rostrata

Moray Eels

family Muraenidae   order Anguilliformes

Moray eels lurk in holes and crevices in rocky areas or coral reefs throughout tropical and temperate seas. Only the head protrudes, ready to strike at any passing prey.

Most moray eels forage at night, seizing fish or octopuses in mouths bristling with backward-curving, fang-like teeth. They also scavenge, and locate their meals with a keen sense of smell. Their prominent nostrils contribute to a gruesome appearance, and vary in style between species.

Ten-foot-long eels do exist, although most average five to six feet. Divers and reef waders fear morays for their unpredictable, aggressive attacks. These unprovoked attacks conflict with stories of snorkelers hand-feeding wild morays. The bite leaves a nasty, jagged wound subject to infection. Throughout their range, morays themselves are eaten, although the flesh can cause a sometimes fatal type of food poisoning known as ciguatera.

A slimy mucus protects the eel's brightly colored or patterned, leathery skin from abrasions. These conspicuous markings set the many species apart.

The green moray, *Gymnothorax funebris,* has a wavy dorsal fin along its back, and is the largest of the

Blue ribbon eel
Rhinomuraena amboinensis

Green moray eel
Gymnothorax funebris

Atlantic morays, reaching lengths of six feet or more. Its blue body appears green through its yellow mucus covering. Ranging from New Jersey to Brazil, it seldom lives deeper than 50 feet. Maria, a record-sized green moray on exhibit in the Aquarium for over 10 years, successfully underwent first-of-its-kind "cataract" surgery to restore lost vision.

The patterned California moray, *Gymnothorax mordax,* which lives in rocky kelp areas, is a food fish of the southern California coast. The three-foot-long spotted moray, *Gymnothorax moringa,* is a smaller species common in the West Indies, from Florida to Brazil. It is a favorite food of green morays. The blackedged moray, *Gymnothorax nigromarginatus,* occurs in the Atlantic, Caribbean and Gulf of Mexico and attains a length of three feet.

The most striking of all morays may dwell among the dazzling reefs of the South Pacific, including the boldly striped, brown and white zebra moray, *Echidna zebra,* which crushes crabs, lobsters and molluscs with its pebble-like teeth.

Ribbon eels of the genus *Rhinomuraena,* from the Indo-Pacific, have widely flaring nostrils and slender, four- to five-foot, boldly colored bodies.

Conger Eels

family Congridae   order Anguilliformes

Conger eels are common along ocean coasts, rocky shores, jetties, piers, tide pools and in wrecks. A few live in deep water. Their rippling dorsal fins, pectoral fins and overhanging jaws distinguish them from other eels.

Large conger eels, up to nine feet in length and weighing 140 pounds, are very powerful and dangerous if provoked. Most feed on crabs, lobsters, shrimps and octopuses, tearing them apart with closely packed, stout teeth.

Many species are known, ranging from the largest, *Conger conger,* a European species valued for its excellent flesh, to little garden eels no longer than three feet. These gentle plankton-eaters sway in the currents with their tails rooted in individual burrows. Large colonies are found in the sandy shallows of the Caribbean, east Atlantic and Gulf of California. The five-foot-long American conger, *Conger oceanicus,* occurs along the Atlantic coast from Cape Cod to South America.

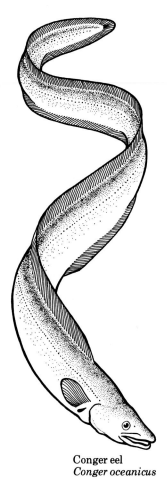

Conger eel
Conger oceanicus

Pikes

family Esocidae   order Salmoniformes

Long favored by anglers, members of this family conceal their mottled bodies in densely weeded rivers and lakes in cool northern regions.

Solitary hunters, pike attack their prey with short, swift lunges. They strike and grasp their victims in their broad snouts, well armed with many, large teeth. Larger species feed on fish, including other pike, salmon and trout, as well as ducklings, small mammals and amphibians. Voracious predators, pike control the populations of many other freshwater animals, including popular sport species, earning the fishermen's nickname "freshwater pirate."

The mighty muskellunge, *Esox masquinongy,* outweighs them all at a record 102 pounds and an angler's maximum of 70 pounds. Smaller muskies are now caught in the Great Lakes watershed where they are rare sport fish prized for their fight, size and excellent flavor.

The smaller northern pike, *Esox lucius,* attains a hefty five feet in its range throughout the northern hemisphere where it has many names: pike, pickerel, jack and snake. In the United States it is a favorite of sport fishermen; in Europe, both anglers and commercial fishermen harvest northern pike.

The smaller grass and chain pickerels occupy the same weedy, stream bed habitats in separate parts of the United States: the two-foot chain pickerel, *Esox niger,* in the east; the foot-long grass pickerel, *Esox americanus vermiculatus,* in the Mississippi Valley and western states.

Juvenile muskellunge
Esox masquinongy

Mudminnows, Alaska Blackfish

family Umbridae   order Salmoniformes

Central mudminnow
Umbra limi

These small, freshwater fishes resemble miniature pikes, and survive harsh conditions lethal to most other species.

The mudminnows, abundant in cool North American lakes, ponds and marshes, live for days and even weeks buried, tail first, in mud. Many endure severe winters in near-frozen states, despite low temperatures and oxygen levels. Reaching three to six inches, members of the genus *Umbra* are an important food for many larger species.

A mudminnow of the frozen north, the nine-inch Alaska blackfish, *Dallia pectoralis,* stalks insect larvae, crustaceans and snails in the brooks, lakes and bogs of the Alaskan tundra north to the Arctic coast. It reportedly withstands freezing in the winter ice, reverting to its normal state when thawed.

Trout, Salmon, Whitefishes, Ciscos

family Salmonidae   order Salmoniformes

Trout and salmon are famous, hard-fighting sport species. They are of great commercial importance, as are their smaller relatives, the whitefishes and ciscos.

Clear, cool fresh waters of the temperate north and Arctic regions suit the sleek, small-scaled trout and salmon. Their eggs travel well, allowing biologists to develop hardy varieties for stocking in streams and lakes throughout the northern hemisphere, far beyond natural haunts. Trout farms alone produce over 300 million pounds of fish annually for both sport and food.

Trout
The beautiful rainbow trout, *Salmo gairdneri,* is native to the western United States, where anglers favor it over all others. Because of its popularity, millions have since been introduced to cold rivers and lakes around the world. Black spots pepper the rainbow's back, tail, fins and the swath of red along each side. Names for rainbow trout include the term "steelhead," which refers to the characteristic silvery body and steely blue head.

Some rainbows migrate. Others live and spawn in cold streams and rivers where they challenge anglers

Rainbow trout
Salmo gairdneri

with legendary fighting and leaping agility. Rainbows
forage on the bottom for invertebrates and small fishes,
or rise to the surface to eat insects or the hopeful
fisherman's hand-tied fly.

Sizes range from four-foot-long, 40-pound ocean
steelhead to the stream anglers' average one-pounder.
Great Lakes rainbows weigh eight to nine pounds, but
do not reproduce in the big lakes, only in the smaller
feeder streams. Hatcheries stock midwest waters with
millions of rainbow fry annually to support the valuable
sport fishery.

Of all the trout, the five-foot-long Atlantic salmon,
Salmo salar, most embodies the name *Salmo,* derived
from the Latin word that means "to leap." Its species
name refers to its ocean habitat: *salar* means "of or
belonging to salt water." It ranges throughout the North
Atlantic Ocean, although in fewer numbers now due to
overfishing, pollution and obstruction of spawning
streams. Atlantic salmon also live in large northern
lakes. Unlike Pacific salmon, adults spawn several
times.

Brown trout, *Salmo trutta,* native to Europe and
widely introduced in northern waters, now abound in
streams and lakes in the upper midwest. Their heavily
spotted, brown bodies average one to two pounds in
stream habitats, ten pounds in lakes.

A prized game fish, the brook trout, *Salvelinus
fontinalis,* occurs naturally throughout the northeastern
United States and Great Lakes where it frequents
shallow coastlines, earning the nickname "coaster."
Also known as "charr" or "brookies," these small, red-
spotted fish average two to three pounds.

Brook trout
Salvelinus fontinalis

Biologists crossbreed brook trout with the larger lake trout to produce the two- to three-pound splake.

Once a major commercial fish in the Great Lakes, lake trout, *Salvelinus namaycush,* flourished until the natural populations were nearly wiped out by overfishing and the sea lamprey. Despite the annual stocking of millions of these deep-water predators since the 1960s, very little natural reproduction occurs in Lake Michigan. In more northern parts of its range, the lake trout breeds in the wild and is still very important commercially, sought for its excellent flavor and large size. The largest of the salmon family native to this region, lake trout may exceed 50 pounds. Their diet consists of alewives, smelt, deepwater sculpins and other forage fish. Average lake trout range from 10 to 20 pounds.

Salmon

The life cycle of the largest member of the family, the salmon, is well known. Pacific salmon begin life in shallow headwaters of cold rivers. Adults return to the streams of their origin after four to seven years of feeding on fish and squid at sea. After tremendous journeys, they lay hundreds of thousands of eggs, and die. Breeding males develop hooked jaws and brighter colors, and in some species, severely humped backs.

Coho and chinook salmon were introduced to the Great Lakes in the 1960s to replace declining lake trout populations. They are important predators of the abundant alewife, and support valuable sport fisheries. Most are stocked from hatcheries since very little natural reproduction occurs.

The coho salmon, *Oncorhynchus kisutch,* grows to over three feet. The black-spotted chinook (or king) salmon, *Oncorhynchus tshawytscha,* averages 20 pounds in the lakes. On the West Coast, the chinook is second in commercial value only to the ocean-dwelling sockeye or red salmon, *Oncorhynchus nerka.* The pink or humpbacked salmon, *Oncorhyncus gorbuscha,* was recently introduced into the Great Lakes where it is rapidly spreading and reproducing.

Whitefishes

Whitefishes are also valuable food fishes but have little worth as sport fishes because they seldom take a hook. Lake whitefish, *Coregonus clupeaformis,* supported a vast fishery in Lake Michigan for many years. The combined effects of the sea lamprey and overfishing nearly eliminated this species in the 1960s. Northern fisheries still meet the demand of fish markets and restaurants. Largest of the whitefishes, these deep-water fish grow to an average weight of four pounds on diets of bottom-dwelling molluscs, insect larvae and shrimp.

Ciscos

As whitefish populations declined, commercial fishermen concentrated on the smaller ciscos or lake herrings. Overfishing resulted in the depletion of many species. Bloaters, *Coregonus hoyi,* are the most commonly caught species and comprise the "chubs" of the Great Lakes smoked fish market.

The 21-inch lake cisco, or lake herring, *Coregonus artedii,* swims in large schools in midwater, feeding on

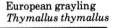
European grayling
Thymallus thymallus

Juvenile chinook salmon
Oncorhynchus tshawytscha

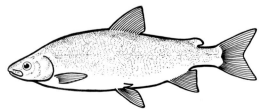

Lake whitefish
Coregonus clupeaformis

plankton and crustaceans. No longer abundant in the lower Great Lakes due to overfishing, lake ciscos are caught in many cold North American lakes for food or sport, and by ice fishermen.

Grayling resemble the larger trouts but are small, averaging one to two pounds. The American species, *Thymallus arcticus,* no longer lives in Lake Michigan. These insect-eating sport fish are important as food to peoples of the Arctic Ocean.

Milkfish
family Chanidae   order Gonorynchiformes

Milkfish
Chanos chanos

One of the world's most important food fish, milkfish, *Chanos chanos,* are cultivated in freshwater ponds throughout southeast Asia, the Philippines and Hawaii. Six-foot-long, fast-swimming adults live at sea most of the year. They enter estuaries and fresh water in large schools to spawn, laying millions of eggs.

Fry are gathered and reared to market size on a diet of plant matter.

Piranhas, Tigerfishes, Pacus, Tetras
family Characidae   order Cypriniformes

This large family of freshwater fishes ranges throughout tropical rivers in Central and South America, Africa and coastal India. Most feed on other fish. Some are vegetarians, while a few eat whatever is available. One of the most diverse groups, it includes the brilliant inch-long tetras, the feared tigerfish and the fierce piranhas.

Piranhas
"The piranha is the most dangerous fish in the Amazon and perhaps in the world," or so older sources claim. Actually, only a few species are dangerous.

Piranhas possess razor-sharp teeth set in powerful jutting jaws. They can snip scalpel-clean bites out of fish or other animals. They often feed in schools, and a hungry pack can easily reduce an animal to bones in minutes. There are numerous reports of fatal attacks on humans, but none of these has been substantiated. In fact, people swim in piranha-infested waters without harm, only fearing attacks when water levels are low and food is scarce.

Piranhas themselves are excellent eating, and are hunted by natives who scoop them into nets or poison

Red-belly piranha
Serrasalmus nattereri

African tigerfish
Hydrocynus vittatus

the water. Large specimens may bite clean through hook and line. Their dried jaws serve to sharpen blow-gun darts or cut tough vines. The word for scissors in the Tupi Indian language is piranha.

Many states now ban the carnivorous species from the pet trade, fearing their destructiveness in local waters if they escape. Reports indicate a breeding population now lives in the Florida Everglades.

Piranhas in captivity become timid, nervous animals, rarely whipping into the feeding frenzies visitors may expect. They grow very large, up to two feet, and live for many years. Several white piranhas, *Serrasalmus rhombeus,* lived at the Aquarium for 26 years.

Piranhas lay adhesive eggs on plants, which the male guards, continuing his vigil even after the fry hatch. The first observed spawning in captivity of piranhas, *Serrasalmus spilopleura,* occurred at the Aquarium in 1959. The young were successfully raised to exhibition size and shared with other aquariums. Other aggressive species on display include the red-belly piranha, *Serrasalmus nattereri,* as well as *Serrasalmus humeralis.*

Tigerfishes

The African version of the piranha reaches much larger proportions. The dagger-toothed, giant tigerfish, *Hydrocynus goliath,* wields its hefty, four-foot, 83-pound body in large West African rivers where reports of attacks on people fuel local fears. More widespread, the smaller, three-foot tigerfish, *Hydrocynus vittatus,* is a highly celebrated sport fish.

Silver dollars

The lovely, irridescent silver dollars may resemble piranhas, but are harmless vegetarian relatives that feed on seeds and the heavy plant growth lining lush, tropical South American rivers. Attractive aquarium fishes, the red-flecked silver dollar, *Metynnis lippincottianus,* and other members of the genera *Myleus* and *Mylossoma* seldom grow to more than eight inches in aquariums. Two-foot-long relatives are favored food fish in native habitats.

Pacus

The blunt-toothed pacus crush nuts and ripe fruits that drop into the South American rivers and floodplains they inhabit, dispersing seeds throughout the rain forest. Natives harpoon the large, tasty pacus, *Colossoma,* when they swim near shore under fruit-laden trees. Also known as tambaqui, the commercially important fish are common in most marketplaces.

Keeled characin
Mylossoma duriventre

Pacu
Colossoma nigripinnis

Tetras

Schools of tiny, brightly colored fishes known as tetras swim in the same South American and African waters housing the ferocious piranha and its relatives. Dazzling jewels of aquariums everywhere, the gentle tetras fascinate the avid hobbist and novice alike with their sociable natures, gift-wrapped in vivid stripes of green, red or blue. Imported or reared commercially for the million-dollar hobbyist trade, tetras breed easily, but the tiny young are difficult to feed and raise in aquariums or small tanks.

Most well known and brilliant of all may be the neon tetra, *Paracheirodon innesi.* In 1936, thousands waited in line at the Aquarium to see the first one ever on display in the United States. One of six collected in South America and shipped to Germany, the lone survivor arrived in New Jersey via the Hindenburg before the airship's ill-fated trip. Flown on to Chicago, "Lonely Lindy" became the first fish to fly all the way from Germany to Chicago. The nearly identical cardinal tetra, *Cheirodon axelrodi,* has a red band from head to tail while the neon's red stripe begins midway.

Since the 1920s, the aquarium world has been flooded with hundreds of varieties of the highly colored fishes from South America, too numerous to list here. A few of

Glowlight tetra
Hemigrammus erythrozonus

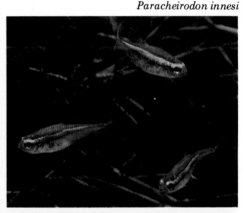

Neon tetra
Paracheirodon innesi

Mexican blind cavefish
Anoptichthys jordani

Congo tetra
Phenacogrammus interruptus

the more brilliant tetras are exhibited in Tributaries, such as the serpae tetra, *Hyphessobrycon callistus.* The slightly larger, head-and-tail light tetra, *Hemigrammus ocellifer,* and glowlight tetra, *Hemigrammus erythrozonus,* live up to their names.

A most unusual tetra, the blind cavefish, *Anoptichthys jordani,* has eye sockets,which are completely covered with skin. The colorless, three-inch-long fish from Mexico lives only in dark, warm water in caves, where vision is useless. The young of the blind tetra have normal eyes that later cloud and shrink. The fish relies on its other sharpened senses to avoid obstacles and find food.

These popular fish have frequently appeared in dimly lit displays since their discovery in the 1930s.

Payara

family Cynodontidae   order Cypriniformes

The payara has a mouthful of huge, fang-like teeth. Its family name translates as "dog tooth." The three-foot-long, narrow-bodied predators inhabit tropical waters in the Amazon basin and Guyana rivers of South America. Aquarium collectors caught several specimens during an expedition to Venezuela in 1982.

Pencilfishes, Spraying Characins

family Lebiasinidae   order Cypriniformes

Slender, brightly colored pencilfishes, *Nannostomus,* linger at the surface of warm, slow-moving rivers in Central and South America. A tailstander, *Nannobrycon eques,* swims head up, feeding on insects at the surface like the other small, banded fishes in this group.

The three-inch spraying characins, *Copella arnoldi,* breed in a most unusual and exhausting manner. The couple repeatedly leap out of the water together, depositing and fertilizing 60 or more eggs on overhanging leaves, a few at a time. The male splashes the eggs every half hour or so until the fry hatch and fall into the water, two or three days later.

The fanning characin, *Pyrrhulina rachoviana,* lays its eggs on a leaf or in a pit. The male continually fans the eggs to provide oxygenated water and remove debris.

Spraying characins
Copella arnoldi

Hatchetfishes

family Gasteropelecidae   order Cypriniformes

To avoid predators or catch flying insects, hatchetfishes
skim over the water like little birds. These extremely
narrow, small, South American fishes look like hatchet
heads, the deep, sharp belly corresponding to the cutting
edge. Strong shoulder muscles in the large breast allow
them to "flap" long pectoral-fin wings as they fly over
the surface for up to nine feet. All other flying fishes only
glide while airborne.

   The common hatchetfish, *Gasteropelecus sternicla,* and
marble hatchetfish, *Carnegiella strigata,* both popular
aquarium animals, exhibit the family's surface lifestyle, pref-
erence for insects and reluctance to breed in aquariums.

Payara
Hydrolycus scromberoides

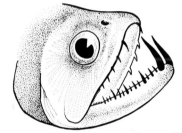

Striped hatchetfish
Gasteropelecus sternicla

Juvenile flagtail characins
Semaprochilodus kneri

Flagtail Characins

family Prochilodontidae   order Cypriniformes

Flashy tails and fins, boldly striped in black, signal the
"small mouths," or bocachicos of South American rivers.
Semaprochilodus insignis is known by aquarists as the
flagtail characin.

   Larger species of these popular tropicals have economic
value as food fish throughout Brazil, Columbia
and Venezuela.

Headstanders

family Chilodontidae   order Cypriniformes

In shallow, marshy tropical rivers in South America, the mud- and plant-eating species in this family swim tail up, mouths nibbling bottom-living algae. The pretty, spotted headstander, *Chilodus punctatus,* is favored by hobbyists, while the abundant, larger members of the family are caught and sold in the marketplace as food.

Spotted headstander
Chilodus punctatus

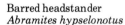
Barred headstander
Abramites hypselonotus

Juvenile spotted leporinus
Leporinus maculatus

Abramites, Leporinus

family Anostomidae   order Cypriniformes

Members of this group swim head down in slow-flowing rivers throughout central South America. They pick small animals or algae out of the mud or graze on algae from rocks. Some have teeth for scraping, but most are toothless. Few are larger than 10 inches.

The stripes of *Anostomus anostomus* disguise the beautiful six-inch fish as it lingers among the weeds and rocks of tropical rivers. Schools of these and other headstanders, including *Abramites hypselonotus,* bob along head down, tilting backwards at times while feeding.

The larger, boldly marked, banded leporinus, *Leporinus fasciatus,* and spotted leporinus, *Leporinus maculatus,* do well in captivity despite "belligerent" natures and a tendency to jump out of tanks.

Bar-lobed hemiodus
Hemiodopsis goeldii and
graceful hemiodus
Hemiodopsis gracilis

Longsnout distichodus
Distichodus lusosso

Distichodus

family Distichodontidae   order Cypriniformes

Large members of this diverse group of plant eaters from
tropical African lakes and rivers, including the
longsnout distochodus, *Distichodus lusosso,* are hunted
for food, some commercially. Ancient Egyptian murals
depict these two-foot-long fish.

The inch-long *Nannocharax ansorgei* and the young
of other species are popular with tropical fish hobbyists.

Hemiodons

family Hemiodontidae   order Cypriniformes

Several of these South American river fishes resemble
pencilfishes in appearance but live on the bottom,
darting between hiding places among stones. Others,
Hemiodus unimaculatus, for example, school in quiet
pools and still backwaters, while a few species prefer
open water and rapids. The silvery aquarium tropical,
Hemiodopsis gracilis, flashes a characteristically red-
streaked tail.

An electric eel,
Electrophorus electricus,
trails telltale air bubbles
shortly after gulping air at
the surface.

Electric Eel

family Electrophoridae   order Cypriniformes

Electric eels, *Electrophorus electricus,* are the most
powerful of the electric fishes, producing a shock of up to
650 volts at one ampere. The strongest discharge stuns
or kills small fish or frogs, which electric eels swallow
whole. It also discourages predators. Weaker discharges
help the nearly blind fish find their way in the turbid
pools and shaded rivers they inhabit in South America.

Most of the electric eel's body, which may exceed six
feet, contains three types of "batteries" made of modified
muscle tissue. The main battery produces the stun
discharge, strong enough to severely shock a person. A
much smaller second battery boosts the main one, while
the third emits repeated signals that are received in pits
covering the fish's head. Any disturbance to this
electrical field warns of obstacles. To maintain its
navigation and detection field, the eel holds its body
fairly rigid. It swims forward or backward by rippling its
long, wavy fin. Two small fins near the head act as
stabilizers.

Muscles modified into
"batteries" produce shocks
that radiate in all
directions. The greatest
effect is within a distance
equal to the fish's length.

Electric eels breathe air and would drown if unable to
rise to the surface about every 15 minutes. Blood vessels
lining their mouths absorb oxygen directly from the air.

Several families of slender, South American freshwater fishes produce weak, electrical impulses. The rapidly fired discharges bounce off of objects, helping the fish avoid obstacles or find smaller fish, crustaceans and insects. Most hunt at night in the warm, murky streams, creeks and rivers they inhabit in Central and South America. A single, long, rippling fin propels them gracefully forward or backward. By day, they linger under plants.

South American Knifefishes

Banded Knifefish

family Gymnotidae   order Cypriniformes

Up to 20 bands mark the two-foot-long banded knifefish, *Gymnotus carapo*. It breathes air at the surface to survive in stagnant tropical water low in oxygen.

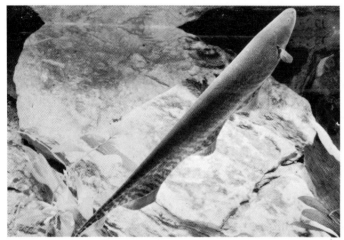

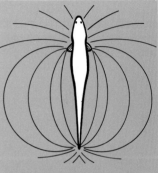

A knifefish detects any disturbances in the electrical field it sets up around its body.
 Impulses generated from the tail region are "read" in special pits in the head.

Banded knifefish, *Gymnotus carapo,* going to the surface for air.

Blackghost knifefish *Apteronotus albifrons*

Ghost Knifefishes

family Apteronotidae   order Cypriniformes

These knifefishes are distinguished by the long, streamer-like fin in the middle of their backs. Many natives believe an evil spirit, or ghost, dwells within the blackghost knifefish, *Apteronotus albifrons*.

Glass knifefish
Eigenmannia virescens

Knifefishes

family Rhamphichthyidae   order Cypriniformes

Several knifefishes are imported as popular aquarium species, including *Rhamphichthys rostratus.* In its native habitat, it forages in the mud for insects with its long, tube-like snout. Adults reach lengths of four and one-half feet, and are caught and eaten.

The smaller glass knifefish, *Eigenmannia virescens,* is nearly transparent, appearing almost invisible in murky backwaters. Adults exhibit a yellow head and green-tinted tail, enhancing their appeal to hobbyists. Collectors seek this species and the shortnosed knifefish, *Hypopomus brevirostris,* which breathes air through modified gills. Certain natives refuse to fish for the latter, however, believing that they are the ghosts of their ancestors.

Minnows, Carps, Goldfish and Relatives

family Cyprinidae   order Cypriniformes

Most people call any small, silvery freshwater fish a minnow. However, the name truly refers to one diverse family of fishes. It includes, besides the prolific minnows, many species of dace, chubs and carp, as well as popular aquarium fishes such as exotic goldfishes, rasboras and barbs. All lack jaw teeth, having strong teeth in their throats instead. Their breeding habits vary, but most shed their eggs on gravel, sand or among plants. A few build nests or attach their eggs to the underside of plants. Many of the males and a few females develop noticeable bumps on their heads during the breeding season.

Minnows, Shiners, Dace and Chubs

Nearly every freshwater habitat in the temperate and
tropical regions of the world, excluding South America
and Australia, houses silvery minnows. Most minnows
feed on small aquatic insects, in many cases helping to
control mosquito populations. They frequently occur in
large numbers and the smaller species are important
food for larger fishes. Popular bait fish, minnows are
farm-raised in ponds for sport fishermen. Favorites
include the three-inch fathead minnow, *Pimephales
promelas,* and four-inch golden shiner, *Notemigonus
crysoleucas.* The golden shiner prefers clear, well-
vegetated ponds or quiet creeks. Because it can also
survive in polluted waters where other species cannot,
biologists use it as an indicator of the water quality of a
particular site.

The emerald shiner, *Notropis atherinoides,* is often the
most abundant fish in the large rivers and lakes it
frequents. Schools form in midwater or near the surface
where the three-inch-long fish feed on insects. Emerald
shiners were formerly very common in the coastal
waters of Lake Michigan. Several hours of dip-netting in
the nearby harbor used to yield enough shiners to serve
as live food for Aquarium exhibits for the entire winter.
One huge school reportedly took over 24 hours to pass
the Adler Planetarium.

A dusky minnow, the central stoneroller, *Campo-
stoma anomalum,* lives in gravel-bottom creeks. The

Emerald shiners *Notropis atherinoides* and
fathead minnow *Pimephales promelas*

Male red shiners, *Notropis
lutrensis,* flaunt the
characteristic bumpy
growths on the head during
the breeding season.

two-inch males excavate nests in the spring by moving small stones and pebbles with their snouts and mouths.

The southern redbelly dace, *Phoxinus erythrogaster,* is one of the most beautifully colored of the minnows. Its black and scarlet stripes are the brightest during the breeding season. This small fish occurs in clear creeks, where it grazes on algae covering submerged objects.

Chubs are larger minnows. The hornyhead chub, *Nocomis biguttatus,* reaches lengths of eight or nine inches.

Rasboras, Danios, Barbs

Colorful Asian minnows include many species that are imported to this country due to their popularity as aquarium fish. Among these is the rasbora, *Rasbora heteromorpha.* Its striking appearance and gentle nature make it a welcome addition to any tropical tank.

Tiger barb
Barbus tetrazona

Rasbora
Rasbora heteromorpha

Redtail shark   *Labeo bicolor*

Rasboras do not have barbels. The similar danios, however, sport small whiskers near their mouths. Many species of danio are well known to aquarists, such as the tiny zebra danio, *Brachydanio rerio,* from India and the four-inch giant danio, *Danio malabaricus.*

Other Asian cyprinids include the barbs, named for the two pairs of barbels that many have near their mouths. One species from India, the mahseer, *Puntius putitora,* grows to over nine feet, and is a favorite food and sport fish. Smaller species, such as the tiger barbs, *Barbus tetrazona,* are beautiful display fish, their crimson or orange fins edging yellow bodies that are boldly striped in black. The tiger barb rarely exceeds three inches. The larger tinfoil barb, *Barbus schwanenfeldii,* up to 14 inches long, is another attractive aquarium species.

The distinctive redtail "shark," *Labeo bicolor,* from Thailand, is named for its coloring and the tall, shark-like fin that characterizes the genus *Labeo.* These small, beautiful fish graze on algae from the walls of their displays, or feed on plants.

Carp

Carp present quite a contrast to the pretty, smaller members of this family. They have been introduced to many continents far-ranging from their native region in Central Asia. Carp are now common in most temperate waters of the world. In many areas, they are cultivated in ponds as an important and cheap food source. A quick growth rate, large size, hardy nature and ability to tolerate low oxygen levels and high temperatures make them an ideal farm species in Asia, Europe and Israel. China leads the world in carp production, where most backyard ponds sport these fish being raised for the family table. There, several species, including the grass carp, *Ctenopharyngodon idella,* and common or mirror carp, *Cyprinus carpio,* often thrive together in the same quiet, weedy pools. They forage on molluscs, crustaceans and vegetation. Their appetite for aquatic plants has led to stocking efforts for the control of weeds.

The Japanese breed a multi-colored hybrid carp for display. The Koi carp, as it is known, may be pure white, gold, red or calico. Carp have been prominent in Japanese art and mythology for centuries, symbolizing virtue, great strength, good health and a long life.

In North America, the carp is regarded by many as a nuisance. It is common in most aquatic habitats, usually soft-bottomed pools of rivers or weedy areas. It stirs up the mud, thus making the water too cloudy for other species. It also feeds on the eggs of other fish, and competes for food with more desirable species. Carp are prolific; each female scatters thousands of eggs on the bottom. They have lived up to 50 years in captivity.

Carp were the first fish on display in the Aquarium when it opened in 1929. They lived in the semi-tropical pool in the rotunda until it was replaced in 1971 by the Coral Reef Exhibit.

Common carp
Cyprinus carpio

Veiltail goldfish
Carassius auratus

Goldfish
Carassius auratus

Goldfish
In the Chicago area, wild carp often interbreed with the closely related wild pond goldfish, *Carassius auratus,* which prefer the same habitat. Goldfish can be distinguished from carp by their lack of barbels.

The natural coloration of goldfish varies from dark grey to greenish gold. These pond goldfish grow to lengths of 14 inches.

Goldfish, like carp, have been introduced nearly worldwide. In the late 1800s, they "escaped" into native

American waters from ponds where they were kept for ornamental purposes. Fishermen furthered their spread by discarding live bait goldfish into lakes and streams.

In some parts of the world, goldfish have been valued for centuries. A Chinese fable from the Chow Dynasty, 750 B.C., tells of a hundred-day drought that parched the earth. Sacrifices were made to Chinese gods, and a well appeared, from which the first goldfish emerged. Then the rains began.

Goldfish have long been collected, cultivated and kept as pets. Exotic varieties of domestic goldfish have been raised in China since the 10th century, in Japan since the 16th century and in the United States only since the 1800s.

Fancy goldfish are usually small, only a few inches long. Countless crossbreedings have resulted in the exaggerated features and dramatic colors that characterize those favored by hobbyists. The veiltail flaunts a lacy, sweeping, three-lobed tail, while the celestial telescopes peer always upwards from their enlarged, bulging eyes. The Chinese are credited with developing the lionhead, which has a head covered by warty growths. It lacks a dorsal fin.

Suckers and Buffalofishes

family Catostomidae   order Cypriniformes

Suckers and buffalofishes are common inhabitants of North American rivers, lakes and ponds. A few species occur in Asia. Most are distinguished by their thick, bristly lips surrounding a downward-pointing mouth.

White sucker
Catostomus commersoni

Smallmouth buffalo *Ictiobus bubalus*

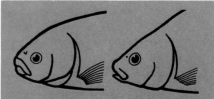

The bigmouth buffalofish, left, is not strictly a bottom-feeder like the smallmouth buffalofish, right, which has a more typical, sucker-like mouth.

The hefty buffalofishes look more like carp than like other suckers. The species name of the bigmouth buffalo, *Ictiobus cyprinellus,* means "small carp." It catches swimming crustaceans in its upturned mouth, unlike the bottom-feeding smallmouth buffalo, *I. bubalus,* which has a more typical sucker-like mouth. Both the three-foot-long bigmouth and its smaller relative are abundant. Considered fine-tasting but bony, they are caught by commercial fishermen throughout the midwest.

Quillbacks, *Carpiodes cyprinus,* closely resemble the larger buffalofishes, but are not considered edible. This species and other carpsuckers in the genus *Carpiodes* prefer quiet pools and slow streams, where they are often the most numerous fishes. Many brandish a long, quill-like ray that extends from the large fin on their backs.

Suckers, *Catostomus,* including the white sucker, *C. commersoni,* usually school near the bottom. Most feed on insects extracted from the mud that they suck up from the bottom. White suckers eat the eggs of other fishes and frequent the spawning streams of salmon and trout, consuming eggs as fast as they are laid. Although bony, their flesh is sweet and firm and is readily marketed, both fresh and salted, in some areas.

The many species of redhorse suckers, genus *Moxostoma,* earn their name from the color of their fins during the breeding season. The river redhorse, *Moxostoma carinatum,* crushes clams in special, large, molar-like teeth far back in its throat.

The northern hog sucker, *Hypentelium nigricans,* lives exclusively on the aquatic young of certain insects, which it finds under stones.

Lake chubsuckers, *Erimyzon sucetta,* are smaller suckers found in heavily vegetated pools and lakes, where they are fed on by largemouth bass and other predators.

Loaches

family Cobitidae   order Cypriniformes

Loaches are small, freshwater fishes that are widespread in Asia and Europe. They inhabit swiftly flowing streams or still pools, often burrowing into sandy bottoms. Many loaches survive in stagnant water by swallowing air at the surface, absorbing the oxygen through their intestines. Their sucker-like mouths suggest their bottom-feeding lifestyle.

Several species of loach discourage predators with sharp, backward pointing spines, one beneath each eye. Among these are many popular aquarium species, including the brightly colored clown loach, *Botia macracantha,* "large spine." This hardy fish is known to live for 25 years or more.

One species, the European weatherfish, *Misgurnus fossilis,* becomes very active just before storms. In parts of Europe it has been kept to serve as a weather prophet.

Clown loach
Botia macracantha

Catfishes roam the world's lakes, rivers and seas. They are carnivorous bottom-feeders, relying on whiskery barbels in their search through murky water for anything small enough to swallow.

Catfishes are most abundant in the Amazon region of South America. Many of these families are well represented in the Aquarium, as are the common North American families.

Most are important food fishes throughout their range, including the African and Asian families, Bagridae and Schilbeidae. These and other more exotic species are seldom exhibited.

Catfishes

North American Catfishes

family Ictaluridae   order Siluriformes

North American catfishes nestle under mudbank overhangs or beneath the protection of submerged tree trunks. Smaller species often seek shelter under rocks or stones. Catfish rely on their eight whiskers to "taste" the bottom while scavenging for any available food.

The largest and best-tasting species, the blue catfish, *Ictalurus furcatus,* and the flathead catfish, *Pylodictis olivaris,* reach lengths of five feet and weights of over 100 pounds.

The channel catfish, *Ictalurus punctatus,* star of the popular "fish fry" in many river communities in the central and eastern states, averages five pounds. Commercial fisheries once yielded fish weighing as much as 30 pounds. Farms now raise millions of pounds annually.

Almost every midwestern pond, stream or lake contains the yellow bullhead, *Ictalurus natalis,* and black bullhead, *Ictalurus melas.* In summer, hundreds of the young school in tight balls near a watchful parent. The tasty bullheads familiar to anglers are not a commercially important species.

Most secretive of all, the stream-dwelling madtom catfishes, *Noturus,* hide under rocks or bottom debris. Many of these small, dull brown catfishes mature at lengths of two to three inches. Several spines in the pectoral fins carry a venom and inflict painful stings.

Channel catfish
Ictalurus punctatus

Brown bullhead
Ictalurus nebulosus

Eurasian Catfishes

family Siluridae   order Siluriformes

A diverse family of catfishes, it includes the largest of all, the ten-foot *Silurus glanis,* called wels in Europe. This immense fish lives in rivers and lakes, as well as the brackish water of the Baltic and Caspian seas, and has a ferocious reputation, reportedly claiming human victims.

By contrast, the miniature glass catfishes, *Kryptopterus,* reach a mere four inches in length. Their transparent bodies reveal every bone and internal organ, and almost disappear against their surroundings.

Glass catfish
Kryptopterus bicirrhus

Juvenile sharkfin catfish
Pangasius sutchi

Sharkfin Catfishes

family Pangasiidae   order Siluriformes

The Asian sharkfin catfishes have short, distinct dorsal fins, reminiscent of sharks. The giant Mekong catfish, *Pangasianodon gigas,* reaches a length of over eight feet and is found only in the Mekong River of Southeast Asia. Other scavenging sharkfin cats, genus *Pangasius,* reach commercial size, but are not always eaten because of a reputation as trash-feeders. However, the same species caught elsewhere may be highly marketed for its fine flavor.

Airbreathing Catfishes
family Clariidae   order Siluriformes

Warm, stagnant lakes and rivers in Africa and Asia
harbor catfishes that survive low oxygen levels by
breathing air. The walking catfish, *Clarius batrachus,*
actually leaves the water, squirming and crawling about
for hours on its two strong pectoral fins (*batrachus*
means "frog"). It survives as long as its gills remain
moist. Breathing by clamping its gill cavities shut to
trap air and water inside, it wriggles hundred of yards
between pools.

Accidentally introduced into Florida, the predatory
walking catfishes now breed and flourish in the warm
climate where food is abundant. Biologists worry that
they will out-compete native species.

In their native habitat, many species are commercially important.

Walking catfish
Clarius batrachus

Shovelmouth catfish
Chaca chaca

Shovelmouth Catfish
family Chacidae   order Siluriformes

The shovelmouth catfish, *Chaca chaca,* is native to fresh
waters of India and Southeast Asia. Rarely moving, its
brownish-black, eight-inch body is easily mistaken for a
piece of wood. With swift short rushes, it captures small
fishes in its cavernous mouth.

Electric Catfish
family Malapteruridae   order Siluriformes

The electric catfish, *Malapterurus electricus,* lives in murky tropical African swamps. It can produce split-second bursts of up to 350 volts of electricity. It may shock again and again to stun its prey or discourage predators, but each charge gets progressively weaker.

Its unique electric organs, made of modified skin tissue, sheath nearly the entire length of the catfish. (All other electric fishes use organs derived from muscles.)

Electric catfishes are caught for food and for use in cure-all charms or potions.

Electric catfish
Malapterurus electricus

The electric catfish wears a "jacket" of electric organs. It emits one of the strongest shocks of the electric fishes, exceeded only by that of the electric eel.

Upside-down catfish
Synodontis nigriventris

Upside-down Catfishes
family Mochokidae   order Siluriformes

Schools of these catfishes often swim upside-down in tropical African rivers. Feeding groups of *Synodontis nigriventris* hang upside down while cleaning algae from the underside of a floating log or stone ledge, yet easily swim upright as well. Few are of commercial importance. The small species, 10 inches or less, are used for bait.

Sea Catfishes

family Ariidae   order Siluriformes

Numerous species of sleek, silvery sea catfishes exist in warm oceans throughout the world. Many enter rivers as well.

Sea catfishes resemble their freshwater relatives, except for an unusual method of caring for the young. The male sea catfish, *Arius felis,* carries dozens of large eggs in its mouth for weeks. There, the young hatch and live for several more weeks, stacked like cordwood. The father feeds them by drawing in water containing food particles, until they swim free as two-inch versions of the adults.

The Aquarium received acclaim for its successful breeding of the North American species in 1972, 1976 and 1978. It occurs naturally on the Atlantic coast from Cape Cod to Panama.

Sea catfish
Arius felis

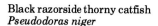

Black razorside thorny catfish
Pseudodoras niger

Thorny Catfishes

family Doradidae   order Siluriformes

Thorny spines cover these secretive catfishes. They hide under fallen logs and stones during the day, becoming active at twilight. One unusual species, the six-inch talking catfish, *Acanthodoras spinosissimus,* produces quite loud grunts and squeaks. When spines in the pectoral fins vibrate against the air bladder, the latter amplifies the sound.

The black razorside thorny catfish, *Pseudodoras niger,* also produces sounds. This species and other doradids are fished commercially in South America.

Banjo Catfishes

family Aspredinidae   order Siluriformes

These dully mottled catfishes are named for their odd
appearance, rather than for any sounds or noises. Active
at night, they lie still during the day among the
vegetation blanketing South American ponds, streams
and coastal river mouths. Most grow to six inches, but a
few species reach lengths of one and one-half feet.

Saddled banjo catfish,
Bunocephalus amarurus,
facing right

Juvenile coral catfish
Plotosus anguillaris

Coral Catfish

family Plotosidae   order Siluriformes

Striped coral catfishes, *Plotosus,* hide by day among
Indo-Pacific coral reefs and turtle grass beds. Their
obvious markings signal a warning to predators that
they carry needle-sharp, venom-laden spines in their
fins.

At night, or in murky water, schools of coral catfish
roam the shallows, entering bays, inlets and rivers as
they forage for food. They steal bait and further annoy
Australian fishermen because their spines inflict very
painful, slow-to-heal wounds and may cause death.

Long-whiskered Catfishes
family Pimelodidae   order Siluriformes

One set of very long barbels marks these Central and South American catfishes. They range in size from the secretive, two-inch dwarf catfishes, *Microglanis,* to the five-foot-long speckled giant catfish, *Pseudopimelodus zungaro.* The huge six-foot *Brachyplatystoma filamentosum,* and other large species are voracious predators of fish and other aquatic animals. For example, one 40-inch redtailed catfish, *Phractocephalus hemiliopterus,* contained a large crab, and the head of a pacu, *Colossoma,* that probably weighed 20 pounds.

Like many South American fishes, some members of this family enter the seasonally flooded forests to feed upon seeds and fruits. The important interrelationship between tropical river fishes and valuable tropical forests only recently has been documented.

Tiger catfish
Pseudoplatystoma fasciatum

Redtailed catfish
Phractocephalus hemiliopterus

Mailed Catfishes

family Callichthyidae   order Siluriformes

Large, bony scales protect the mailed catfish from
predators. They also prevent drying during the fish's
forays over land. A few species, such as *Hoplosternum,*
crawl, hop or jump rather quickly, one individual
covering almost 300 feet in two hours. They swallow air,
pass it into the intestines and absorb it into their
bloodstream as an alternate means of getting oxygen.

Often brightly marked, some of the popular aquarium
species school in slow-moving or stagnant rivers in
South America and Panama. These small, two- to eight-
inch bottom-dwellers feed on any available food.

Mailed catfish
Hoplosternum sp.

Suckermouth Catfishes

family Loricariidae   order Siluriformes

Tough, bony plates armor the suckermouth catfishes.
They are found in many different habitats in central
South America, from stagnant pools to rushing rivers.
Their thick lips form a sucker mouth on the underside of
the head that allows these fish to hang on to objects in
almost any position. With small rasping teeth, they
gnaw algae from rocks or graze on larger aquatic plants.
In the Aquarium, they keep exhibit tanks well groomed.

Few look alike, the many species varying greatly in
color and shape.

The stick suckermouths, *Farlowella,* avoid detection
by mimicking sticks on river bottoms. The brown,
mottled and spotted sailfin suckermouth, *Ptery-
goplichthys,* blends in with dead leaves. *Xenocara,*
which usually hides beneath rocks, shows bright blue
spots on a black body.

Suckermouth catfish
Peckoltia sp.

Lizardfishes

family Synodontidae   order Myctophiformes

Lizardfish perch on their fins on the sandy sea floor, their scaly, pointed heads contributing to their reptilian appearance. They lie in wait, darting upwards to catch small fish. Like other species, the sand diver, *Synodus intermedius,* quickly buries itself up to its eyes when disturbed. It is the most common species in the Bahamas.

Lizardfish inhabit the shallow, inshore waters of tropical oceans. Divers and snorkelers frequently see them near patch reefs and coral heads. The foot-long red lizardfish, *Synodus synodus,* is widely distributed on both sides of the Atlantic.

Lizardfish are related to the lanternfishes, family Myctophidae. Lanternfish are the most abundant, best known and most often seen of the bizarre, deep-sea fishes.

Sand diver
Synodus intermedius

Trout-perch
Percopsis omiscomaycus

Trout-perch

family Percopsidae   order Percopsiformes

Trout-perch feed on aquatic insects on the silty bottoms of large rivers and lakes. In turn, many larger fish feed on these small fish.

Only two species of these entirely North American fishes are known. The trout-perch, *Percopsis omiscomaycus,* occurs throughout Canada and the Great Lakes region. Usually in shallow water, it is occasionally found as deep as two hundred feet.

The sand roller, *Percopsis transmontana,* inhabits fresh waters in the Pacific northwest.

Pirate Perch

family Aphredoderidae   order Percopsiformes

Pirate perch
Aphredoderus sayanus

The black or dusky purple pirate perch, *Aphredoderus sayanus,* lives in swamps and ponds throughout the eastern United States, which are well-littered with organic debris. It is small, about four inches long, and is not commonly encountered. Biologists note the unusual migration of its vent from near its tail when young to a spot under its throat when fully grown.

Cavefishes

family Amblyopsidae   order Percopsiformes

Northern cavefish
Amblyopsis spelaea

Cavefish are tiny inhabitants of the subterranean streams or surface swamps of the southern states. Most are blind, their eyes covered by skin. The young are born with eyes that see, but skin grows over them as they mature. Adults navigate and find food using special sense organs arranged in rows on their heads, bodies and tails.

The northern cavefish, *Amblyopsis spelaea,* from the Mammoth Caves of Kentucky, is colorless, as are most species.

The swampfish, or ricefish, *Chologaster cornuta,* retains its color and has small but functional eyes. It lives above ground in cypress swamps and streams along the Atlantic coast of the United States.

Cod, Haddock, Burbot

family Gadidae   order Gadiformes

Cod and their relatives are among the most valuable food fishes in the world. With the exception of the freshwater burbot, they are all fishes of the northern seas. Cod live near shore in winter, going into deep water as temperatures rise. Many stay near the bottom. They spawn in late fall and winter, the females laying millions of eggs that float at the surface and are spread by wind and tide.

The Atlantic cod, *Gadus morhua,* and haddock, *Melanogrammus aeglefinus,* are the mainstay of the north Atlantic fisheries. The Atlantic cod is the largest species and has been fished commercially for centuries due to its keeping qualities when dried or salted. It has the chin barbel and fin placement typical of the family. The smaller haddock is known as "finnan haddie" when served smoked. Its young frequently seek shelter among the trailing, stinging tentacles of jellyfish, as do young whiting, *Merlangius merlangus.* As adults, these two species occupy different habitats and vary in feeding habits. Haddock live near the bottom, feeding on brittle stars, shellfish and worms. Whiting, and the equally valuable North Atlantic pollock, *Pollachius virens,* feed on young cod in midwater, or eat bottom-dwelling fishes, such as sand eels.

The bluish gray, cod-like hakes migrate towards the surface of colder oceans to feed at night, returning to deeper water by day. They feed on schooling fishes and squids, and in turn are consumed by larger marine predators including whales, seals and sea lions. The European hake, *Merluccius merluccius,* and Pacific hake, *M. productus,* are commercially important species.

The Pacific cod, *Gadus macrocephalus,* receives little attention in American fisheries. It is one of Japan's most important food fishes, where it is called "tara."

Burbot
Lota lota

Atlantic cod
Gadus morhua

Red hake
Urophycis chuss

The burbot, *Lota lota,* is the only exclusively freshwater cod species. It is a coldwater fish known to live as deep as 700 feet in the Great Lakes. In winter, it ventures into shallower water to spawn, laying eggs on the bottom. Burbot feed voraciously on other fish, including yellow perch, whitefish and ciscos. In Europe, burbot is considered a great delicacy, and is one of several fishes known as "poor man's lobster." There is little demand for it in the United States, but increased marketing efforts are encouraging the consumption of this underutilized species.

Eelpouts
family Zoarcidae   order Gadiformes

In 1936, the Aquarium's director, Walter Chute, photographed a female Atlantic ocean pout, *Macrozoarces americanus,* guarding her eggs in one of the display tanks. It documented for the first time that this species was an egglayer. Others were known to bear live young, the European eelpout, *Zoarces vivaparus,* for example.

1936 photograph of an ocean pout, *Macrozoarces americanus,* guarding her eggs in an Aquarium exhibit.

Eelpouts are drab-colored, cold-ocean fishes, that grow to lengths of two feet. A seemingly continuous fin runs from the back of the head around the tail and forward to a point under the throat. Their pouting countenance derives from thick, fleshy lips and a considerable overbite. Bottom-dwellers, eelpouts hide in rocky crevices, coming out to feed on crabs and molluscs. They are common from the shallows to great depths.

Gulf toadfish
Opsanus beta

Toadfishes

family Batrachoididae   order Batrachoidiformes

Toadfish hide by day on the bottom among debris,
blending well with their background. They prowl sand
flats and shallows at night, feeding voraciously on
resting fish. Nurse sharks and other marine predators,
in turn, feed on toadfishes. Common in tropical and
temperate seas, estuaries and some rivers, they are often
found in ankle-deep water. A few live at great depths.

Some species have hollow spines in their fins and on
their gill covers. Each is connected to a venom gland at
its base. The venom causes extreme pain, but is not fatal
to man. Belligerent and quick to bite, toadfishes rarely
flee from danger. Many grunt or croak at night or at any
disturbance.

The shallow-water, fifteen-inch oyster toadfish,
Opsanus tau, has the characteristic flattened head and
mouthful of teeth. This species ranges from Cape Cod to
Cuba in the Atlantic.

Anglerfishes

The anglers usually lie concealed on the sea floor,
difficult to see because of their coloring and lumpy
shapes. They entice prey near their cavernous mouths
by wriggling a single "fishing pole" tipped with a fleshy
lure. The realistic lure is actually a modified dorsal spine
known as an *illicium,* a Latin term meaning "seductive,
enticing."

Curious fish fooled by the lure seldom live long enough
to learn their mistake. Anglers snap up prey with a
lightning-fast gulp that belies their sedentary nature.
Voracious eaters, they also slowly stalk prey by crawling
on their stout, arm-like fins. Anglers seldom swim.

Deep-sea anglers, from depths of one thousand to three
thousand feet, often carry luminescent lures. The tiny
males of some species become parasitic. They permanently attach to the much larger females, assuring each
of a mate in the vast, black void of the oceans' depths.
Others function as males and females at the same time,
thus able to mate with either sex that comes along. They
do not fertilize their own eggs, however.

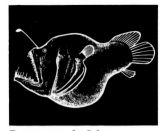

Deep-sea anglerfish
Melanocetus murrayi

Goosefishes

family Lophiidae   order Lophiiformes

The ugly countenance of the goosefish, the largest of the
anglerfishes, is unmistakable. Its enormous mouth
bristles with many sharp, thorn-like teeth. Fleshy tabs
covering the immense, flattened head break up its outline
as it lies camouflaged on the sea floor. It swallows anything that approaches, including small sharks, turtles,
fishes, squids, crabs or even diving seabirds.

Goosefishes live in all temperate and tropical oceans,
where some grow to lengths of five feet. The American
goosefish, *Lophius americanus,* ranges from New
England to Brazil, and from the tideline to depths of
2,000 feet. Long considered excellent eating in Europe
and Japan, goosefish are gaining in popularity in the
United States under the market name of "monkfish."

Goosefish
Lophius americanus

Frogfishes

family Antennaridae   order Lophiiformes

Their scientific name, translated from the Latin word for antennae, refers to the efficient lure most frogfish use to attract prey. But it is their unusual fins, shaped like frog legs, and their frog-like lunges for prey, that give these anglers their most popular name.

Most lead sedentary lives on the bottom, where they may be mistaken for clumps of bright sponges or algae-covered rocks. Some are mottled, striped, spotted or solid yellow, black, brown or even bright orange. A few slowly change colors. In the tropical Atlantic, the sargassum-fish, *Histrio histrio,* (meaning "actor, actor"), perfectly matches its habitat of clumps of seaweed floating at the surface.

Polka-dot batfish
Ogcocephalus radiatus

Frogfish
Antennarius sp.

Batfishes

family Ogcocephalidae   order Lophiiformes

Perhaps the oddest looking of the anglers, batfishes crawl sluggishly along the ocean bottom, usually in deeper water. When hungry, these fish display a short lure that appears from behind a flap of skin and vibrates either to the right or left of the small mouth.

Flattened and warty-skinned, the polka-dot batfish *Ogcocephalus radiatus,* lives among weeds in the shallows of the Caribbean.

Halfbeak
Dermogenys pusillus

Halfbeaks and Flying Fishes

family Exocoetidae   order Atheriniformes

The lower jaw of the halfbeak juts out like a sword. The
upper jaw is of normal length. Males of the three-inch
halfbeak, *Dermogenys pusillus,* wrestle each other with
locked jaws until exhausted. In Thailand, these
pugnacious fish are bred and matched in exhibition
contests.

Most halfbeaks are larger than *Dermogenys,*
averaging 18 inches in length. They school at the
surface of tropical and temperate seas, as well as rivers
in Asia.

Many halfbeaks leap but fail to glide, lacking the large
fins necessary for this feat. Their well-known relatives,
the flyingfishes, soar for long distances on extended
"wings" that are held rigid, not flapped. They do not
truly fly. Flyingfish accelerate below the surface before
taking to the air. A few scull the water, or "tail-walk,"
with a lengthened lower tail fin to maintain their speed
and altitude.

Needlefishes

family Belonidae   order Atheriniformes

Needlefishes brandish long, sharply toothed beaks.
They feed voraciously on other fish at the surface of
warm and temperate seas. A few species live in fresh
water, including the foot-long aquarium species
Xenetodon cancila from Asia.

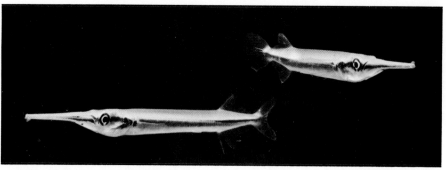

Juvenile silver needlefish
Xenetodon cancila

Needlefishes frequently leap into the air and "tail-walk" for short distances, particularly when disturbed by bright lights or a passing boat. The largest species, the five-foot-long houndfish, *Tylosurus crocodilus,* has been called a "living javelin." People in boats have been severely injured when impaled by its pointed beak as the fish hurtled out of the water. Found worldwide, it frequents shallow, coastal waters. It is also known as "poor man's marlin" because of its leaping behavior when hooked.

Ricefishes
family Oryziatidae   order Atheriniformes

In the rice fields of lowland Japan, olive-brown ricefishes, *Oryzias latipes,* feed on mosquito larvae. Domestic aquarium varieties are usually rose-colored with golden bellies. The young hatch from clusters of eggs that hang below the female for a short time before she transfers them to plants. Because of their rapid development, these fish have been the subject of classic fish embryology studies.

Killifishes
family Cyprinodontidae   order Atheriniformes

These small, egglaying fishes resemble minnows and small carps, but have teeth lining their jaws. Variously called toothcarps, or killifishes, they are also known as topminnows because they school at the surface, feeding on insects. Widely distributed in fresh and brackish water, toothcarps range worldwide, with the exception of Australia, in tropical and temperate areas.

Many species are popular aquarium fish, the males flaunting more vivid colors and patterns than the often drab females. Many are easily collected in estuaries or freshwater ponds in North America. The pretty flagfish,

Blackstripe topminnow
Fundulus notatus

Pair of redspotted killifish,
Aphyosemion cognatum,
shown mating, below.

Jordanella floridae, lives only in ponds in Florida.
Thriving in eelgrass beds, tide pools and marshes along
the east coast are both the sheepshead minnow,
Cyprinodon variegatus, and smaller mummichog or
killifish, *Fundulus heteroclitus.* These hardy species, like
other family members, survive high temperatures, low
oxygen levels and, in a few cases, drought, sometimes
living partially buried in the sand.

Several South American and African species are
particularly adapted to regions of alternating, intense
dry and rainy seasons. The adults spawn when the
temporary puddles and river pools they inhabit begin to
evaporate at the onset of the annual drought. The eggs
remain buried in the mud through the dry season,
during which the parents die. Months later, when the
yearly rains bring moisture, the young develop and
hatch. These fishes, known as annuals, include the
African lyretails, *Aphyosemion,* and the Argentine
pearlfish, *Cynolebias.* Aquarists breed these colorful fish
by recreating their harsh environmental conditions, and
even ship ready-to-hatch eggs in the peat moss or sand
in which they were laid. Add water and *voilà:* instant fish.

Each divided eye of the four-eyed fish, *Anableps anableps,* allows it to see equally well in the air and in water.

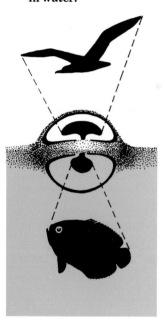

Four-eyed Fishes

family Anablepidae　order Atheriniformes

The four-eyed fish lies at the surface, simultaneously watching above and below for prey and predators. Each protruding eyeball of the four-eyed fish, *Anableps anableps,* is divided across the center into two separate eyes. The top half sees accurately in air as the fish swims with its head at the water line, body hanging slightly below. The lower half peers through the coastal and estuarine waters of Central and South America. Locals call it *cuatro ojos,* or "four eyes."

Protectively colored, it is hard to see from above, the outline of its body being broken up by a bright stripe. Viewed from below, the light belly blends in with the surface. It frequently bobs beneath the surface to moisten its unusual upper eyes, exposed to the air. On shorelines, it frequently climbs entirely out of the water, resting on mangrove tree roots.

Livebearers

family Poeciliidae　order Atheriniformes

Guppies, mollies, swordtails and platys are, besides goldfish, perhaps the most well known of the beautiful aquarium fishes. Prolific breeders, these small toothcarps bear live young, unlike the egglaying toothcarps, Cyprinodontidae.

Strikingly colored males fertilize the eggs internally, using a tube formed by the anal fin. This gonopodium, as it is called, distinguishes the different species. One mating often yields several broods.

Pike topminnow
Belonesox belizanus

Male and female common guppies
Poecilia reticulata

Least mosquitofish
Heterandria formosa

Livebearing toothcarps occur in warm regions in North and South America. Many species have been introduced worldwide because of their hearty appetites for mosquito larvae. Typical of these, the surface-feeding mosquitofish, *Gambusia affinis,* thrives in heavily weeded streams and marshes. Its adaptability in some cases has resulted in its survival at the expense of native species. One species of mosquitofish, the inch-long *Heterandria formosa,* is the tiniest of the livebearers.

Dwarfing its miniature relatives, the eight-inch pike topminnow, *Belonesox belizanus,* is a Central American livebearer that looks, acts and feeds like a miniature pike. It lurks near the surface of mudstained backwaters and pools, and tolerates fresh or salt water.

Many livebearers adapt readily to confinement, particularly the well-known guppy, or "million fish," *Poecilia reticulata.* These two-inch fish are named for Reverend J. L. Guppy, who first discovered them on the island of Trinidad in the 1800s.

Guppies are native to fresh- and brackish-water habitats in the Caribbean and Amazon basin. Now found worldwide, their cosmopolitan distribution is the result of mosquito control measures and the release of pet fish into local waters.

Male and female
butterfly goodeids
Ameca splendens

The closely related mollies are also crossbred to produce different colors and forms. The males bear the characteristic, large dorsal fin. In the wild, the common sailfin molly, *Poecilia latipinna,* is multi-colored. This species inhabits the coastal areas and river mouths of the southeastern United States and Mexico. The domestic black varieties do not occur naturally. Other mollies sought for their attractiveness include *Poecilia mexicana.*

An all-female population of livebearers lives in Mexico, the Amazon mollies, *Poecilia formosa.* These females must mate with males of closely related species to produce offspring, which are always female.

Attractive swordtails and platys, *Xiphophorus,* have a range of natural colors and forms that have been

Male and female sailfin mollies
Poecilia latipinna

Platy
Xiphophorus variatus

Female swordtail, double sword variety
Xiphophorus helleri

enhanced by aquarists. Medical scientists also crossbreed them for use in genetic studies and cancer research. Female swordtails, *Xiphophorus helleri,* lack the flamboyant tail carried by the males. Some change sex, however, gradually altering color and shape to become fully functioning males.

From high altitude lakes and streams in Mexico are imported a related family of popular aquarium livebearers, Goodeidae. The pretty *Ameca splendens* readily breed and rear their broods of 20 or more young.

Rainbowfishes

family Melanotaeniidae   order Atheriniformes

These peaceful, schooling freshwater fishes from Australia and New Zealand decorate aquariums with their brilliant hues. Rainbowfishes thrive in well-lit aquariums, laying eggs that attach to plants until the young hatch.

Their natural habitats are diverse, ranging from desert springs to lakes, ponds, swamps and brackish mangrove forests. Many linger in sunlit waters, earning a regional nickname, sunfish.

Rainbowfishes are abundant, and are important food for other fishes. In parts of New Guinea, they are eaten by natives after being sun-dried and salted.

Freshwater fishes from these continents are difficult to collect and import because of the vast, rugged terrain separating their remote habitats from populated areas.

Black-edged rainbowfish
Melanotaenia nigrans

Silversides

family Atherinidae   order Atheriniformes

Silversides school in tropical and temperate seas, usually close to shore and near the surface. A few live in clear, fresh water. Most of these fairly small fish flash a metallic silver band on each side.

The California grunion, *Leuresthes tenuis,* has extraordinary breeding habits. During the highest spring tides, numerous pairs of breeding grunion flop ashore and deposit eggs in the sand. These remain

Hardhead silverside
Atherinomorus stipes

Male and female Celebes rainbowfish   *Telmatherina ladigesi*

buried until the next high tides wash over them. The young hatch almost immediately and ride to sea on the waves.

A beautiful species that inhabits only certain fresh waters in Indonesia also graces many aquariums, the tiny Celebes rainbowfish, *Telmatherina ladigesi.*

In North American lakes and streams, the four-inch brook silverside, *Labidesthes sicculus,* is an important forage fish for larger species, as is its marine counterpart, the hardhead silverside, *Atherinomorus stipes.* Huge schools of the latter are common in the Caribbean.

Pinecone Fishes

family Monocentridae   order Beryciformes

Pinecone fish, *Monocentris japonicus,* are named for the heavy, overlapping scales covering their rounded bodies. Sharp spines on their backs alternate left and right, and they are further protected by strong pelvic spines. These five-inch fish live in dark water at depths of 100 to 600 feet off the Pacific coasts of Japan and Australia.

Pockets on either side of the lower jaw contain symbiotic bacteria that produce a considerable glow, hence one species' name, port-and-starboard-light fish. The bacteria frequently die in aquariums, where their luminescence is seldom seen.

Pinecone fish are caught in trawls by Japanese commercial fishermen, and are eaten fried or roasted with vinegar, or in soup.

Pinecone fish
Monocentris japonicus

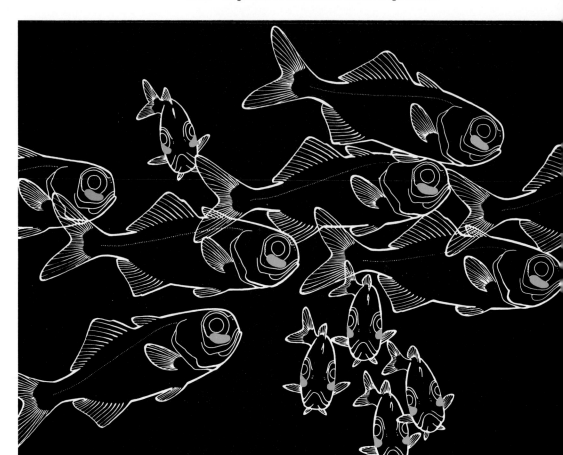

Eerie, blue-green lights flicker at night as schools of flashlight fish feed near deep reefs, close to rocky crevices and overhangs. The family name means "abnormal eye."

Flashlight Fishes

family Anomalopidae   order Beryciformes

Many fishes that live in dimly lit or deep, dark water possess lights, the glow often produced by symbiotic bacteria. Flashlight fishes are unique among these because they can, in effect, turn on and off their powerful "headlights," the brightest carried by any animal.

Pockets beneath each eye contain billions of bacteria that use sugar and oxygen from the fish's blood, radiating light as a by-product.

Each species has a different mechanism for covering these constantly shining lights. *Photoblepharon palpebratus,* from the Red Sea and Indian Ocean, raises a black "eye-lid" over each pocket. Another species from the same area, *Anomalops katoptron,* rotates the entire pocket inward. The Caribbean flashlight fish, *Kryptophanaron alfredi,* uses both methods: the former for quick flashes, the latter for longer dark periods.

These secretive fish shun well-lit waters, hiding by day at depths of 300 feet or more. They become most active on moonless nights. Their bright lights, or "lantern eyes," lure prey, but also predators. By "blinking" and darting away in the darkness, flashlight fish zig and zag their way to safety, leaving the confused predator behind. Their lights also help them to navigate and communicate.

The glowing bacteria will survive without the fish for several hours. Indonesian fishermen attach them above their hooks to lure fish or suspend baskets of living flashlight fish below their boats as reusable lures.

Squirrelfishes, Soldierfishes
family Holocentridae   order Beryciformes

Dark waters in warm seas harbor nocturnal squirrel-fishes and soldierfishes. By day, these secretive reef fishes hide their crimson and red hues under ledges and in caves and crevices. At night, however, their true numbers become apparent as large schools forage over coral reefs, feeding on smaller fish and invertebrates. In poorly lit waters, their red colors look black, rendering them nearly invisible.

Flashlight fish, *Photoblepharon palpebratus,* with pocket of bacteria exposed.

Bacteria exposed...covered

Each species turns its "headlights" on and off in a different fashion. *Anomalops* rotates each glowing pocket of bacteria inward to cut off the light.

Reef squirrelfish
Holocentrus coruscus

Mating pair of blackbar soldierfish
Myripristis jacobus

Shrimpfish
Aeoliscus strigatus

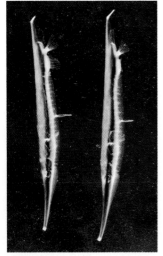

Large, squirrel-like eyes, spines and rough scales characterize members of this family, some of which reach lengths of two feet. Despite their spines, several appear in seafood markets, including *Myripristis amaenus,* known as *menpachi* in Hawaii.

Many squirrelfishes and soldierfishes grunt, croak or click loudly, at least during courtship. Their swirling mating dances in exhibits at the Aquarium bring these normally elusive fishes into full view.

Shrimpfishes

family Centriscidae   order Beryciformes

Lengthwise black stripes help camouflage the shrimpfish, *Aeoliscus strigatus,* as it hovers head down between the long black spines of sea urchins. Other species of these small Indo-Pacific fishes exhibit this same habit of swimming vertically.

A protective covering of thin, bony plates produces a sharp ridge under the belly, and for this reason, Australians call *Centriscus scutatus* the razorfish.

See page 18
Aquatic Adaptations.

Seahorses and Pipefishes

family Syngnathidae   order Gasterosteiformes

Harlequin pipefish
Dunkerocampus dactyliophorus,
facing right.

Described as having "the head of a horse, the pouch of a kangaroo and the tail of a monkey," the curious-looking seahorse is a favorite of visitors.

In the shallows of warm seas, seahorses linger among sea grasses, their protective coloring rendering them nearly undetectable. Slow, weak swimmers, they usually anchor themselves by curling their tails around plants or gorgonians. Seahorses eat by sucking tiny animals into their narrow tube mouths with astonishing speed and accuracy.

Rings of bony "armor" encase seahorses. They remain upright and rigid even while swimming. Small fins vibrating as fast as 35 times a second propel them slowly through the water. A nod or turn of the head changes direction.

Perhaps the seahorse's most unusual characteristic is the incubation of the eggs by the male in his unique brood pouch. The young hatch from eggs laid by the female in this special fold of skin. Live, miniature seahorses then pop from the father's protruding belly.

Seahorses display different color phases, some species becoming bright orange, red, yellow, brown or black. They range in size from the one-and-one-half-inch dwarf seahorse, *Hippocampus zosterae,* to the giant seahorse, *H. kuda,* that averages eight inches but sometimes reaches a length of one foot.

Seahorses were long valued for medicinal purposes — dried or ground as an aphrodisiac, used as a cure for

Juvenile dwarf seahorse
Hippocampus zosterae

baldness or to relieve pain and dipped alive in oil of roses to treat chills and fever.

The closely related pipefishes look like straightened seahorses as they swim horizontally through turtle grass and algae. Known to enter brackish and even fresh water, they otherwise share many of the same traits as seahorses, including the male brood pouch. In the Pacific, gaudy harlequin pipefish, *Dunckerocampus dactyliophorus,* hover beneath overhanging coral heads in the shallows. The only open-sea species is the sargassum pipefish, *Syngnathus pelagicus,* which hides in the floating seaweed beds of the Atlantic.

Sticklebacks

family Gasterosteidae   order Gasterosteiformes

Territorial, red-bellied male sticklebacks build elaborate nests among plants. Leaves and bits of vegetation are cemented together with special, sticky threads. After coaxing females to enter the nest and lay eggs, the attentive fathers remain to care for the young. They often maintain several nests at one time.

Sticklebacks breed throughout cooler waters in the northern hemisphere. Many thrive in both fresh and salt water, for example, the widespread, threespine stickleback, *Gasterosteus aculeatus.*

Male 15-spine stickleback,
Spinachia spinachia, in nest

Brook stickleback
Culaea inconstans

The stickleback trademark is a row of movable spines near the head. The number varies between species. The small brook stickleback, *Culaea inconstans,* has four to six spines, but usually five. This is a freshwater species common to the Great Lakes region and farther north. A similar European species became famous as Dickens' "Tittlebat" in *Pickwick Papers.*

Their formidable spines fail to discourage birds, otters, trout, perch, pike and other predators that feed heavily on these small fishes. Sticklebacks harbor many parasites, including one that must be eaten by birds to complete its life cycle. Sticklebacks in turn consume the fry and eggs of other fishes, often desirable sport species.

Swamp Eels
family Synbranchidae   order Synbranchiformes

Swamp eels are airbreathing fishes known from stagnant backwaters and lagoons in Asia, Africa and Central and South America. Despite a naked, snake-like appearance, they are true fish. Many survive long, dry periods by burrowing in the mud, staying inactive until their pools are restored by seasonal rains.

One widespread species in Central and South America, the spotted eel, *Synbranchus marmoratus,* travels long distances over land, perhaps in search of water. It survives by filling its gill chamber with air. Another, the rice eel, *Monopterus alba,* is caught for food in rice paddies and ditches throughout Asia as well as in Hawaii where it was introduced.

Spotted synbranchid eel
Synbranchus marmoratus

Scorpionfishes, Rockfishes
family Scorpaenidae   order Perciformes

Among this large family of marine fishes are the venom-laden scorpionfishes, the commercially valuable deepwater rockfishes and the magnificent tropical lionfishes.

Known as turkeyfish or lionfish, the brilliantly marked Indo-Pacific fishes in the genus *Pterois* gracefully and fearlessly linger near reefs. Spines protruding from the elaborate fins carry a potent venom. These can cause near-fatal injuries to those foolish enough to approach too closely.

At least one species, *Pterois volitans,* purposefully presents its dorsal spines towards threatening objects. With fins spread wide, lionfish maneuver smaller reef fish into corners, then swallow them with a lightning-fast gulp.

Scorpionfishes lead more sedentary lives on the bottom, camouflaged among shells, rocks and algae. When alarmed, the spotted scorpionfish, *Scorpaena plumieri*, warns of its venomous nature by flashing a vivid pattern on its pectoral fins. The venom glands are at the base of each dorsal spine. A bright orange Mediterranean species, *Scorpaena scrofa*, is a main ingredient in the well-known French fish soup, *bouillabaisse*.

Spotfin lionfish
Pterois antennata

Treefish
Sebastes serriceps

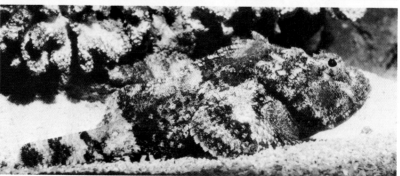

Spotted scorpionfish
Scorpaena plumieri

Many other species in this family are commercially valuable, including the savory redfish, *Sebastes marinus,* one of several species marketed as ocean perch. Commercial trawlers from many countries seek these fish at depths of 300 to 700 feet. Bottom-dwellers by day, they feed at night in the open seas, where they are eaten, in turn, by halibut, cod and whales.

Many Pacific species in the same genus are known as rockfishes because they inhabit rocky areas and crevices, usually near the bottom. Most are red, a color that looks black and blends in with dark, dimly lit deep water. Trawlers haul in the valuable Pacific ocean perch, *S. alutus,* the bocaccio, *S. paucispinis,* and a West Coast version of the popular Atlantic red snapper known as yelloweye rockfish, *S. ruberrimus.*

A closely related family of fishes, Synanceiidae, includes the most venomous fish of all, the deadly stonefish. A swimmer died two hours after stepping on a half-buried fish. Seldom moving, it resembles a rock on the sea floor, its camouflage enhanced by the algae and debris that cover its back.

Tiger rockfish
Sebastes nigrocinctus

Vermillion rockfish
Sebastes miniatus

Horned searobin
Bellator militaris

Searobins

family Triglidae   order Perciformes

Skinny "fingers" under a searobin's exceptionally broad pectoral fins probe the ocean floor for food. It feeds on crustaceans as well as bottom-living fishes.

Searobins, also known as gurnards, frequent sandy or rocky coastal habitats in tropical and temperate oceans.

The armored searobin, *Peristedion miniatum,* wears bright red armor of thick scales and bony plates. It lives deep in the Atlantic off the east coast of the United States. The northern searobin, *Prionotus carolinus,* is more abundant in shallower water from Canada to Venezuela.

Flying gurnards, Dactylopteridae, could be mistaken for searobins in behavior and appearance if it were not for their broader heads and larger sail-like fins. Despite reports attributing aerial feats to these "broad-winged" fishes, they limit any occasional glides to the water.

Flying gurnard
Dactylopterus volitans

Greenlings

family Hexagrammidae   order Perciformes

Greenlings rarely venture far from the rocky ocean floor of the North Pacific coast.

The mottled patterns of the kelp greenling, *Hexagrammos decagrammus,* are barely discernible among shallow rocky reefs and kelp beds. Despite this, these fish are preyed upon by trout, salmon, sharks, sea birds and sea lions.

The largest of these savory marine fishes is the five-foot-long lingcod, *Ophiodon elongatus*. Commercial trawlers and sport fishermen catch them in the intertidal zone as well as at great depths.

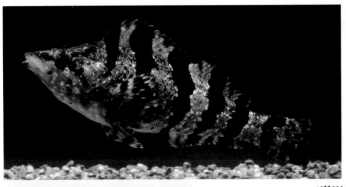

Painted greenling
Oxylebius pictus

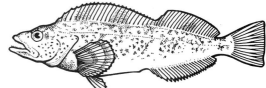

Lingcod
Ophiodon elongatus

Sea raven eggs laid in an Aquarium exhibit in 1982.

Sea raven
Hemitripterus americanus

Sculpins

family Cottidae   order Perciformes

Sculpins are abundant in cooler regions. They are found in freshwater streams and from the shoreline to great depths in both the Atlantic and Pacific Oceans.

Most are small, the exceptions including the hefty red Irish lord, *Hemilepidotus hemilepidotus*. This 20-inch predator searches the shallows of the American Pacific coast for crabs, barnacles and mussels, when not buried in the sand. Even larger, the deeper-water cabezon, *Scorpaenichthys marmoratus*, exceeds 30 inches.

An Atlantic cousin of moderate size inhabits rocky areas from Chesapeake Bay to Labrador. The sea raven, *Hemitripterus americanus,* bristles with prickly flaps of skin that give it an untidy appearance. Its striking yellows and reds are unmistakable.

Just over three inches long, the tidepool sculpin, *Oligocottus maculosus,* is a familiar sight to Pacific coast beachcombers. These red or brown "rock pool johnnies" dart between rocks, peering upwards from eyes high on their prominent heads.

Their freshwater counterpart, the mottled sculpin, *Cottus bairdi,* consumes trout and salmon eggs and those of other species that spawn in clear, rocky streams and lakes. The slimy sculpin, *C. cognatus,* occurs in the Great Lakes region in deep water. In true sculpin style, the male excavates nests under stones, then guards the eggs laid by the female on the underside of the roof.

Tidepool sculpin
Oligocottus maculosus

Mottled sculpin
Cottus bairdi

The dramatic fin of the marine sailfin sculpin, *Nautichthys oculofasciatus,* makes this fish seem larger than it really is. The species name describes the black streak that camouflages its large eyes.

The Greek word *rhampos,* part of the name of the grunt sculpin, *Rhamphocottus richardsoni,* means "a crooked beak," referring to its distinctive snout. With it, this peculiar-looking little fish searches in crevices and between barnacles for small animals. Jumping or crawling over rocks and seaweed on fingerlike fins, it only swims when in a real hurry. It grunts loudly when removed from the water. Baby grunt sculpins hatched in 1981 at the Aquarium.

Poachers
family Agonidae   order Perciformes

In arctic and cold seas, particularly the North Pacific, sea poachers dwell on sandy or muddy bottoms, often at great depths. The many-whiskered sturgeon poacher, *Agonus acipenserinus,* is one of the largest at one foot in length. Poachers forage for worms and crustaceans, themselves protected by rows of heavy bony plates.

Sturgeon poacher
Agonus acipenserinus

Snailfishes, Lumpfishes
family Cyclopteridae   order Perciformes

Suckers formed by fins on the bellies of these marine fishes grip rocks on the sea floor. Most live in cold seas from the tidelines to great depths.

Lumpy growths or spines cover the lumpsuckers. Europeans and Russians trawl in the North Atlantic for the two-foot lumpfish, *Cyclopterus lumpus.* The eggs are

Spotted snailfish
Liparis callyodon

also favored and are marketed as caviar. Male lumpfish feverishly guard the eggs that are laid in a large, spongy clump on the bottom, earning the nickname "sea hen."

The smaller snailfishes are covered by a smooth, jelly-like skin. The widespread Atlantic striped seasnail, *Liparis liparis*, displays a characteristic mottled, barred or spotted pattern.

Lumpfish, *Cyclopterus lumpus,* guarding white clump of eggs, right.

Indian glassfish
Chanda ranga

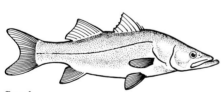

Snook
Centropomus undecimalis

Snooks, Glassfish

family Centropomidae   order Perciformes

This diverse group of fishes includes many of great food value as well as smaller species popular as pets.

They range worldwide in tropical seas, brackish estuaries and freshwater rivers. The sleek snooks, or *robalos* in Spanish, entice sport fishermen throughout the Caribbean, tropical Atlantic and Pacific. Reaching lengths of four and one-half feet, the common Florida snook, *Centropomus undecimalis,* prefers the shallows and is often abundant in mangroves in Florida.

In African coastal waters, estuaries and the Nile river system, one species reaches six feet or more. Ancient Egyptians revered the Nile perch, *Lates niloticus,* burying mummified fish in tombs along the Nile. Throughout Africa, members of this genus are often the most important single food fish and rank as prized, hard-fighting sport fish.

Miniature, by contrast, are the four-inch glassfish from fresh and brackish waters in Africa, Asia and Australia. The nearly transparent *Chanda ranga* is the most familiar of these pretty little aquarium fish.

Temperate Basses

family Percichthyidae   order Perciformes

A family of fishes closely related to the sea basses and groupers includes the giant sea bass of the Pacific coast, *Stereolepis gigas.* Adults frequent rocky sea floors below kelp beds, and are great sport fish. Few approach the record size of one specimen weighing 557 pounds and measuring 81 inches, which must have been a very old fish. A 434-pound sea bass was known to be 75 years old.

Wreckfish, *Polyprion americanus,* are reclusive cousins that haunt wrecks, often in deep water. Young wreckfish live among floating debris and algae from which they dart out after prey.

A more illustrious relative native to Atlantic waters is the famous game fish known as "stripey," the striped bass, *Morone saxatilis.* Its popularity led to its successful

Striped bass
Morone saxatilis

introduction to Pacific coastal waters in the late 1800s. On both coasts, striped bass enter freshwater rivers to spawn. This active, inshore predator has been known to reach lengths of 50 inches.

White perch, *Morone americana,* also enter fresh water along the Atlantic coast and have become landlocked far inland. They, too, are important sport fish. The closely related white bass, *Morone chrysops,* and yellow bass, *Morone mississippiensis,* are strictly freshwater species found in the eastern and midwestern regions of the country. (Although called "perch" and "bass," these fishes should not be confused with the well-known yellow perch, family Percidae, and small- and largemouth basses, family Centrarchidae.)

Sea basses and Groupers

family Serranidae   order Perciformes

Groupers and sea basses are startling, quick-change artists that bewilder other tropical reef-dwellers as they instantly slip from one color phase or pattern to another. They match coral backgrounds as a disguise while resting or lying in wait for prey. Many display dark stripes or dots superimposed on a pale background to signal alarm.

The Nassau grouper, *Epinephelus striatus,* which ranges from North Carolina to Brazil, is one of the more outgoing of these normally shy and reclusive fishes. Divers easily recognize its black-saddled, tan and brown patterns. A popular pastime is the taming and hand-

Tobaccofish
Serranus tabacarius

Vermillion grouper
Epinephelus miniatus,
near soft corals.

feeding of wild groupers that inhabit shallow reefs near
dive resorts. As with other reef fish caught for their fine
flavor, they have been involved in cases of fatal food
poisoning. The Nassau grouper is a junior member of the
family, reaching a length of only four feet.

The largest grouper reigns unchallenged in the Indo-
Pacific and Barrier Reef where alert swimmers watch for
its huge shadow. The Queensland grouper, *Epinephelus
lanceolatus,* weighs up to half a ton and grows to be 12
feet long, inspiring undocumented reports of Jonah-like
swallowings of skindivers. A voracious carnivore that
stalks its prey, it has been known to follow divers as
though to attack.

The slightly smaller jewfish, *Epinephelus itajara,* gets
its name from the Spanish word for any large grouper,
guasa. Jewfish linger near wrecks and caves, feeding on
spiny lobsters, fishes, sea turtles and anything that can
be engulfed in their huge mouths. Sports records boast of
an eight-foot, 551-pound specimen caught on tackle. The
hefty proportions of Joshua, a six-and-one-half-foot, 450-
pound jewfish, amazed Aquarium visitors from 1973 to
1978. Estimated to be 28 years old when caught, Joshua
was probably only half-grown.

Jewfish
Epinephelus itajara

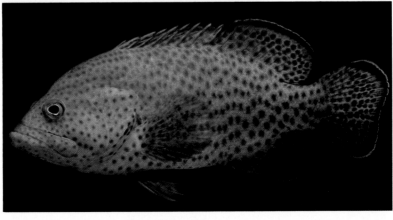

Red hind
Epinephalus guttatus

Jewfish, like many other sea basses and groupers, change sex as they age. Young fish are female, becoming functional males later in life. The young females often live in harems, usually tended by one male. Should the male leave, the senior female becomes male after several weeks.

Vivid colors and striking patterns adorn many of the smaller species favored for display. The beautiful Caribbean coney, *Epinephelus fulvus,* and rock hind, *Epinephelus adscensionis,* are sought for that reason, as are graysbys, *Epinephelus cruentatus,* and butter hamlets, *Hypoplectus unicolor,* also from the tropical Atlantic and Caribbean. There are many dazzling Pacific species, including the vermillion grouper, *Epinephelus miniatus.*

Leaflip soapfish
Pogonoperca punctata

Soapfishes

family Grammistidae   order Perciformes

The slimy skin of a soapfish turns water foamy and sudsy, and repels predators with its lethal, bitter-tasting toxin. Vivid stripes or patterns warn of danger to any that might otherwise make a meal of one of these tropical marine fish.

Even so, the Atlantic greater soapfish, *Rypticus saponaceus,* hides in shallow, rocky crevices by day, while the Indo-Pacific golden-striped soapfish, *Grammistes sexlineatus,* stays in and around coral heads.

Juvenile golden-striped soapfish
Grammistes sexlineatus

Fairy basslet
Gramma loreto

Dottyback
Pseudochromis sp.

Basslets

family Grammidae   order Perciformes

The festive colors of the little fairy basslet, *Gramma loreto,* may alert larger fishes to its cleaning service.

Skin and mouth parasites troubling other fish provide the basslets with a meal. These normally shy fishes prefer reef caves and crevices, where they always orient towards a hard surface, even if it means turning upside-down.

Coral reefs in Indo-Pacific waters house similar small fishes, known as dottybacks, of the closely related families, Pseudochromidae and Pseudogrammidae.

Mimic roundhead,
Calloplesiops altivelis,
facing right

Mimic Roundheads

family Plesiopidae   order Perciformes

Most reef fish hide when threatened, but not the mimic roundhead, *Calloplesiops altivelis.* It intimidates and deceives hungry fish by imitating the whitespeckled moray eel, *Gymnothorax meleagris,* a distinctly marked predator.

When alarmed, the mimic roundhead ducks into a crevice, leaving the end of its body exposed, including the fake eyespot below the dorsal fin. The predator is fooled, mistaking the tail-end of the fish for the head of an aggressive moray eel.

Roundheads frequent shallow inshore reefs and rocky areas throughout the Indo-Pacific.

Tigerperches

family Theraponidae   order Perciformes

Dark stripes break up the body line of these fishes that inhabit the warm coastal waters and estuaries of the Indo-Pacific. Curving lines distinguish the frequently exhibited crescent tigerperch, *Therapon jarbua.* Both it and the trumpeter tigerperch or croaker, *Pelates quadrilineatus,* perform a noisy serenade of grunts and croaks, audible even when out of water.

Adults reach moderate lengths of eight to twelve inches and are efficient predators in the shallows, sand flats and grassy beds they inhabit.

Crescent tigerperch
Therapon jarbua

Aholeholes

family Kuhliidae   order Perciformes

Aholeholes (ah-holy-holy), *Kuhlia sandvicensis,* are
schooling fishes of Hawaiian coral reefs. Silvery in color,
their Hawaiian name means "sparkling." They are good
eating whether served raw, dried, salted or broiled on hot
coals. Fishermen catch them at night when they leave
crevices to graze on algae. Younger fish frequent
tidepools and shallow coastal waters, entering estuaries
and river mouths.

   Aholeholes and their relatives have been likened in
appearance to North American sunfishes and basses,
Centrarchidae. Black bands on the tails of some,
particularly *Kuhlia taeniura,* are responsible for the
popular name of flagtail fish. Species of this family are
known throughout the Indo-Pacific.

Aholehole
Kuhlia sandvicensis

Bluegills
Lepomis macrochirus

Black crappie
Pomoxis nigromaculatus

Basses, Crappies, Sunfishes

family Centrarchidae   order Perciformes

Lurking in weed beds and under ledges, these freshwater predators peer out and lunge for smaller fish or a fisherman's bait. Largemouth and smallmouth bass, crappies, sunfishes and bluegills, native to North America, now thrive worldwide due to their popularity as game and forage fish.

The angler's record largemouth bass, *Micropterus salmoides,* caught in 1932, weighed twenty-two and one-half pounds and measured thirty-two and one-half inches. The largemouth is the largest member of the sunfish family and tolerates a variety of habitats, from swamps to weedy river backwaters or clear lakes. Smaller fishes, including bluegills, sustain the hearty appetite of this large predator. The bass' mouth extends behind the eye, distinguishing it from its highly sought relative, the smallmouth.

Sportsmen claim that the smallmouth bass, *Micropterus dolomieui,* is, pound for pound, the gamest fish that swims. The record weight is 12 pounds at a length of 27 inches, although the average length is around one foot. Somewhat selective about its surroundings, smallmouth bass prefer clear, gravelly rivers, streams or lakes.

Like all sunfishes, the rock bass, *Ambloplites rupestris,* single-mindedly guards the eggs laid in a nest that the male fans out of the gravel. Females are chased away by the guardian fathers after depositing their eggs. A red gleam in the eye of the rock bass identifies this robust species as well as the warmouth sunfish, *Lepomis gulosus.*

Crappies provide good sport fishing and tasty panfried meals throughout their range, expanded from the eastern states across the entire country. The white crappie, *Pomoxis annularis,* occurs in all but the smallest ponds and streams, and is able to tolerate silty and weedy conditions. The smaller black crappie, *Pomoxis nigromaculatus,* is most abundant in clearer water, usually among aquatic plants.

The bountiful sunfishes include important forage species. Members in the genus *Lepomis* all display a

Rock bass
Ambloplites rupestris

The mouth of the smallmouth bass, *Micropterus dolomieui,* does not extend beyond the eye.

long gill flap, either spotted or ringed with color. A dark blue patch on each gill cover distinguishes the bluegill, *Lepomis macrochirus,* while an orange flap edged in white marks the longear sunfish, *Lepomis megalotis.* The pumpkinseed, *Lepomis gibbosus,* flaunts wavy, blue cheek paint and orange blotches. Colors become more exaggerated during the breeding season.

Bigeye
Priacanthus sp.

Bigeyes

family Priacanthidae   order Perciformes

Bigeyes are fishes of tropical reefs. They feed at night, hiding among corals or in crevices during the day. In poorly lit waters, their scarlet bodies appear nearly black, and their large eyes gather what little light is available. Both the Pacific goggle-eye, *Priacanthus hamrur,* and the Atlantic bigeye, *Priacanthus arenatus,* reach two feet in length.

In Hawaii, where the bigeye, *Priacanthus cruentatus,* is called *a-we-o-we-o* (ah-vayo-vayo), natives once believed its appearance in abundance foretold the approaching death of royalty. The same species is called glasseye in the Caribbean.

Cardinalfishes

family Apogonidae   order Perciformes

Thousands of small cardinalfishes swarm from coral head to coral head throughout tropical seas. These three- to four-inch fishes are important food for larger reef fishes.

The flamefish, *Apogon maculatus,* and other scarlet species frequent shallow reefs, where they hide during the day. Those with brown and olive-green patterns, including the round cardinalfish, *Sphaeramia orbicularis,* live in the murky waters of mangrove swamps.

One species, the conchfish, *Astrapogon stellatus,* lives within the mantle cavity of the Caribbean queen conch, *Strombus gigas.* Other cardinalfish in this genus seek shelter in uninhabited shells or small caves.

Some cardinalfishes are thought to be mouthbrooders. Parents either carry eggs in their mouths full time or pick up the brood at the first sign of danger.

Orbiculate cardinalfish
Sphaeramia nematopterus

Perch, Walleye, Darters

family Percidae   order Perciformes

Yellow perch are the mainstay of the Great Lakes commercial fisheries. Over half of the total 1980 yield was the golden-bodied, black-barred, *Perca flavescens,* valued at $17 million. Star of the local fish fry, this small, tasty fish excites sport fishermen including those who brave the elements to fish through the ice.

Recently, their numbers have declined, in part due to overfishing and pollution. Also, perch faced stiff competition from the introduced alewife. This species ate young emerald shiners, a favorite food of perch that is now rare in the Great Lakes. In addition, because they can strain very small organisms from the water, alewives competed directly with shiners for food. With cleaner lakes and with alewives now held in check by lake trout and salmon, perch are making a comeback.

Perch originally occurred only in the eastern United States, but their popularity led to an expanded range. A good-size perch weighs about one pound at a length of one foot.

The walleye, *Stizostedion vitreum,* averages several pounds heavier. It was once a favored food fish of the early settlers and natives of the midwest. A popular sport fish, it and the slightly smaller sauger, *Stizostedion canadense,* are making a comeback in Lake Erie where they were once commercially important.

Tiny darters are at the other end of the food chain. Found virtually in every North American freshwater

Yellow perch
Perca flavescens

Walleye
Stizostedion vitreum

Orangethroat darter
Etheostoma spectabile

habitat west of the Rockies, the numerous species are food for larger fishes. Many are well adapted to living on the gravelly bottoms of fast-flowing streams, darting from rock to rock, feeding on young aquatic insects. Rainbow darters, *Etheostoma caeruleum,* brilliantly colored during the breeding season, are called by some the prettiest of the North American fishes.

Tilefishes

family Malacanthidae order Perciformes

The tilefishes, or blanquillos, are a family of bottom-living fishes that inhabit warm seas. The sand tilefish, *Malacanthus plumieri,* excavates an extensive burrow in the sand and rubble into which it dives headfirst at the least disturbance. In the wild, the fish cautiously leaves its watchful post near the opening to feed on bottom-dwelling fishes and crustaceans.

A deepwater species, the tilefish, *Lopholatilus chamaeleonticeps,* from the Atlantic and Gulf of Mexico, is fished for its excellent flavor, both fresh and smoked. Shortly after the discovery of the east coast population in the 1800s, the tilefish was nearly wiped out by a natural mixing of colder water with the warm water it required. For many years, few of these valuable fish were caught. They are currently fished on a small scale.

Peppermint sand tilefish *Hoplolatilus* sp.

Bluefish

family Pomatomidae   order Perciformes

The bluefish, *Pomatomus saltatrix,* is a swift, fierce marine predator, sometimes killing many more fish than it eats. The young are called snapper blues because their mouths are constantly snapping as they search for food. Packs follow the migrating schools of smaller fishes — anchovies, sardines, menhaden, shads, mullets — throughout their range in the Atlantic.

Sport and commercial fishermen work offshore waters to pull in the tough fighter, valued for its excellent flavor. Bluefish reach lengths of four feet and weigh 27 pounds. Their bluish-green color and well-armed jaws are unmistakable.

Cobia

family Rachycentridae   order Perciformes

At six feet, 150 pounds, the adult cobia, *Rachycentron canadum,* ranks as one of the larger marine predators. Its diet includes fish, squids and shrimps as well as crabs, hence its nickname, "crab-eater."

Cobias hunt the open waters, shorelines and estuaries of nearly all tropical oceans. Three silvery bands interrupt their dark sides, the stripes resembling those on the trousers of a sergeant, thus another name, "sergeantfish."

Cobia
Rachycentron canadum

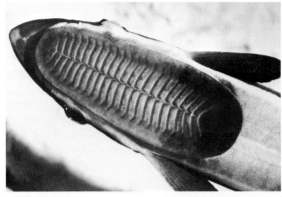

The ridges across the remora's powerful suction disc create a strong vacuum when raised, allowing it to catch rides on larger marine animals.

The grip is released when the remora swims forward, tightened when it slides backward, thus a fast-swimming host won't dislodge the hitchhiker.

Sharksucker
Echeneis naucrates

Remoras

family Echeneidae   order Perciformes

Remoras, also called sharksuckers, hitchhike on larger fishes throughout tropical seas, but can swim freely as well. Visitors often mistake the slim remora riding a nurse shark for a baby shark. A strong suction disc on the remora's head firmly grips the skin of a shark, whale, larger fish, shell of a turtle or even the side of a boat.

The largest, the yard-long remora, *Echeneis naucrates,* prefers sharks, while *Remora australis* is called whalesucker for the company it keeps. When its host feeds, the remora will detach and pick up the scraps. Several species act as cleaners, eating troublesome skin parasites.

Fishermen used to tie a strong line to a ring around a remora's tail and release it near a sea turtle. The remora attached itself so tightly that the turtle could be reeled in and captured.

Their holding powers are legendary. Ancient Romans told of sailing ships detained by the drag of remoras attached to the hulls. They blamed remoras for allowing enemy ships to overcome the vessels of Emperor Caligula and Mark Antony, causing their respective death and defeat. The Latin word *remora* means "one who holds back" and *Echeneis* means "holding ships back" in Greek.

Jacks, Pompanos

family Carangidae   order Perciformes

This diverse family of fast fishes includes racers of the open ocean. Many species are swift and efficient marine predators, capable of maintaining great speeds for long periods of time.

Crevalle and horse-eye jacks, *Caranx*, exhibit sleek bodies, rounded foreheads and sickle-shaped fins, typical of speedy swimmers. Sharp, bony ridges reinforce the tail for fast swimming, and are noticeable on many jacks. These species reach lengths of 30 to 40 inches, and are great sport to catch, although sometimes poor eating. The same can be said for the smaller bar jacks, *Caranx ruber*, called the "passing jack" in the Bahamas because of the large schools that cruise by in the summer.

Black-banded, golden jacks, *Gnathanodon speciosus*, from the Indo-Pacific, are solid yellow when young. During their youth, they behave like the pilot fish, *Naucrates ductor*, which, according to legend, would lead ships to their destination, or guide large fish to food sources. Actually, pilotfish keep close to vessels and other animals to await scraps and handouts, rather than to act as navigators.

Stunning blue bands on the sides of the rainbow runner, *Elagatis bipinnulata*, set it apart from other runners. A great-tasting, hard-fighting sport fish, it is widespread in the tropical Atlantic and Indo-Pacific.

Amberjacks, *Seriola*, up to six feet long, are efficient predators of the open sea. In the Pacific, they challenge

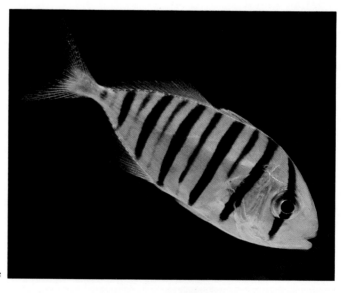

Juvenile golden jack
Gnathanodon speciosus

saltwater anglers as well as commercial fishermen. The angler's record weighed in at 177 pounds. Although good eating, an Atlantic species, *Seriola dumerili,* has frequently caused ciguatera, a type of food poisoning. This species is known by the dark band through its eyes.

Another streamlined species that shares the commercial and sport fisherman's interest is the Pacific jack mackerel, *Trachurus symmetricus.* The related horse mackerel, *T. trachurus,* of the Atlantic, sustains fisheries off the coasts of Africa and the Mediterranean. The young of both spend their early lives within the deadly tentacles of jellyfish.

The 18-inch Florida pompano, *Trachinotus carolinus,* may be the most prized species of fish sold in seafood markets.

The permit, *Trachinotus falcatus,* inhabits shallow Atlantic waters near reefs and sandy flats. Adults rate as excellent sport fish and grow to be 43 inches long. Young feed on small crustaceans in sheltered waters, expanding their diet as they mature to include molluscs and sea urchins.

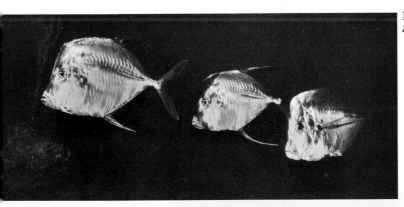

Lookdown
Selene vomer

Black jack
Caranx lugubris

Waders around shallow sandy areas may see schooling palometas, *Trachinotus goodei,* surrounding their feet, nibbling on any molluscs kicked loose in the sand.

Other Atlantic species include foot-long, silvery lookdowns, *Selene vomer,* that are so thin they nearly disappear when viewed head on. Schooling near the surface, they peer ever downward over large mouths.

Streaming fins trail behind young African pompanos and other threadfins, *Alectis.* The resemblance to jellyfish tentacles may provide protection from predators. As the fish get older and reach adult lengths of three feet, their fins appear much shorter.

Snappers

family Lutjanidae   order Perciformes

Many kinds of snappers live in shallow tropical seas, often occurring in great numbers. Restful by day, snappers usually hunt at night, feeding heavily on smaller fishes caught in their large, canine teeth. In turn, these marine predators are valuable food fish, particularly the favored red snapper, *Lutjanus campechanus.* As with many reef fishes, a few have been known to cause food poisoning when caught in certain areas at particular times of the year.

Schoolmaster
Lutjanus apodus

Emperor snapper
Lutjanus sebae

Some snappers reach lengths of three feet. Most live near shore, close to the bottom. Mangroves and tidal creeks are nurseries for the young and home for several species, including the drab gray snapper, *Lutjanus griseus,* and schoolmaster, *Lutjanus apodus,* both of the Atlantic.

By contrast, the beautiful Indo-Pacific emperor snapper, *Lutjanus sebae,* exhibits the mahogany shown by the more colorful species, which may also have yellow and green in their wardrobe. A stunning snapper is the blue-and-orange-streaked threadfin snapper, *Symphorichthys spilurus,* its trailing, streamer-like fins edged in brilliant gold.

Juvenile blue-lined threadfin snapper
Symphorichthys spilurus

Tripletails

family Lobotidae   order Perciformes

Young tripletails, *Lobotes surinamensis,* imitate mangrove leaves floating at the surface, and are common in patches of sargassum weed. Unlike the more elusive adults, juveniles are commonly seen in shallow coastal waters of warm and tropical seas. The illusion of three tails is created by the two large fins that extend as long as the real tail.

Several small species enter fresh and brackish waters in the Indo-Pacific, including the pretty, four-banded tigerfish, *Datnoides quadrifasciatus.*

Juvenile four-banded tigerfish
Datnoides quadrifasciatus

Yellowfin mojarra
Gerres cinereus

Mojarras

family Gerreidae   order Perciformes

In the shallows of tropical mangrove swamps and tidal creeks, small silvery mojarras scoop up mouthfuls of sand to sift out tiny invertebrates. The Atlantic yellowfin mojarra, *Gerres cinereus,* is known in clear reef areas as well as brackish coves.

Grunts

family Haemulidae   order Perciformes

Tropical reef fish known for the sound produced when they grind their throat teeth together are appropriately called grunts. The nearby air bladder amplifies the croaking loud enough to be heard when these popular sport and food fish are pulled on deck. Their Spanish name, *ronco,* means "to snore." A school of grunts playing around the bottom of an anchored boat on a still, tropical night makes enough noise to wake the sleeping crew, according to one report.

Grunts rest in large groups near reefs during the day, moving out at dusk to forage the adjacent sand flats for shrimps, worms, molluscs and small fish. The black margate, *Anisotremus surinamensis,* sometimes feeds on long-spine sea urchins, *Diadema,* that also move out from reefs to graze in turtle grass beds.

In the Atlantic and Caribbean, beautiful French grunts, *Haemulon flavolineatum,* and blue-striped grunts, *H. sciurus,* are among those that approach each other with wide-open mouths. The curious face-to-face display may involve courtship or territorial behavior.

Margate
Haemulon album

School of french grunts
Haemulon flavolineatum

Their mouths are bright red inside; *haemulon* means
"bloody gums." Vivid stripes on many of these schooling
fishes confuse a predator trying to single out one
individual from the blurring mass of a fleeing group.

The young of the brilliant yellow and black porkfish,
Anisotremus virginicus, look different from the parents,
their conspicuous stripes signalling to other fish that
they clean parasites from skin and teeth.

Most colorful of all are the species that inhabit the
Indo-Pacific. Known as "clowns of the reef," young
sweetlips, *Gaterin,* parade and cavort in their bold
patterns, which will change as they approach adulthood.
The brown and white splotches of the juvenile clown
sweetlips, *Gaterin chaetodonoides,* differ so drastically
from the brown freckles of the grey adult that biologists
once classified them as different species. Popular
aquarium fishes, they grow to over a foot and one-half
in length.

Juvenile clown sweetlips
Gaterin chaetodonoides

Adult porkfish
Anisotremus virginicus

Porgies

family Sparidae   order Perciformes

Porgies and sea breams have long been favored for food. The ancient Greeks fished for them and the name porgy derives from their word for these tasty fishes, *pagr.*

Several species inhabit cooler waters off the coast of North America, although they are most abundant in the tropical waters around South Africa. There, the mussel cracker, *Sparodon durbanensis,* scours the shallows for hard-shelled animals, which it crushes in its molar-like teeth.

Most also exhibit the large, buck teeth that are the distinguishing family characteristic. A few species use them to crop large amounts of algae.

Sheepshead
Archosargus probatocephalus

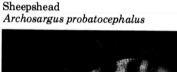

Juvenile scup
Stenotomus chrysops

The distinctive teeth of the sheepshead are unmistakable.

One look at the prominent teeth of the sheepshead, *Archosargus probatocephalus,* explains its name. This northern species inhabits coastal Atlantic waters where it is sought by anglers and commercial fishermen who also value the scup, *Stenotomus chrysops.* Its sharp spines can cause painful punctures.

Another excellent seafood species is the two-foot jolthead porgy, *Calamus bajonado.* It feeds on sea urchins, molluscs and crustaceans inhabiting the reefs of the west Atlantic. Most *Calamus* are inshore fishes named for some aspect of their appearance, for example, the saucereye porgy, *Calamus calamus.*

A large red porgy, the red tai, *Pagrus major,* is a sacred fish in Japan, always depicted in illustrations of the fish god. One of the most important food fishes, it is marketed live, fresh, frozen and spice-cured.

Croakers, Drums

family Sciaenidae   order Perciformes

The din created by thousands of croakers twanging muscles against their air bladders once hid submarines. Before the development of sophisticated equipment, enemy ships could not detect each other's operational noises, or might mistake the sounds of the fish for that of another submerged vessel.

Croakers drum loudest during the breeding season and at night. Some gather in one place and harmonize for unknown reasons. Since many live in murky estuarine waters, their sounds may aid in navigation and communication.

Croakers have sizable ear stones, otoliths, which have long been collected as "lucky stones," as evidenced by those found near ancient camps of native American Indians.

Most croakers are fishes of the tropical and temperate seas. A few species enter fresh water and one, the freshwater drum, *Aplodinotus grunniens,* lives its entire life in rivers from Canada to Guatemala. Its diet, like that of most croakers, is bottom-dwelling molluscs, fishes and crustaceans, which it locates with the aid of barbels.

Warm, shallow bays and coastal waters house the Atlantic croaker, *Micropogonias undulatus,* and spot, *Leiostomus xanthurus.*

High-hat
Equetus acuminatus

Freshwater drum
Aplodinotus grunniens

Black drum *Pogonias cromis*

Larger croakers include the surfcaster's favorite, the red drum, *Sciaenops ocellatus,* once recorded at 83 pounds.

The black drum of the western Atlantic, *Pogonias cromis,* reaches lengths of six feet. As with most other drums and croakers, black drums have flattened bellies and chin barbels, adaptations suggesting their bottom-feeding lifestyle.

Mightiest of all is the rare totuava, *Cynoscion macdonaldi,* which, until recently, flourished at sizes of 225 pounds in the Gulf of California. Closely related to their giant cousin are other valuable food and sport fishes, such as the six-foot California white seabass, *Astractoscion nobilis,* and Atlantic weakfish, or common seatrout, *Cynoscion regalis.* Weakfishes are so called because their mouths are easily torn by a hook. They are also known by the name squeteague.

Ribbonfish, or cubbyus, *Equetus,* are striking in appearance, their tall fins enhancing otherwise small forms. The angle of the dorsal fin suggests one name, jackknife fish. Disruptive dark bands encircle them horizontally and mask the rather large eyes. Their tropical Atlantic habitats include shallow turtle grass beds and sand flats near rocky hiding places.

Goatfishes
family Mullidae   order Perciformes

Bewhiskered goatfishes probe sandy and muddy sea floors with two long sensitive feelers located under their chins. They forage for small worms, shrimps and crabs in the shallows of warm and cool seas.

Most are small. Few exceed lengths of 20 inches. The brilliant colors of some are even more startling when

Golden goatfish
Pseudupeneus cyclostomus

they rapidly change. Goatfishes may also change color
from day to night.

Red mullets, as many species are known, bring high
prices. They have been savored by seafood connoisseurs
since the days of the ancient Romans. In Hawaii, one
species, *Upeneus arge,* is known as the "nightmare
weke" (vecky) because it is hallucinogenic if eaten.

Fingerfishes
family Monodactylidae   order Perciformes

Twice as tall as it is long, the nine-inch fingerfish,
Monodactylus sebae, typifies this deep-bodied family of
tropical Pacific fishes. Dark bands run through its eyes
and from tip to tip of its exaggerated fins. Small schools
are a common sight near docks and mangrove roots, in
coastal waters, estuaries and occasionally in rivers.
Many are imported for the aquarium trade, particularly
Monodactylus argenteus. They are also known as
moonfish, diamondfish, kitefish and fingerfish
(*monodactylus* means "one finger").

Banded fingerfish
Monodactylus sebae

Sweepers

family Pempheridae   order Perciformes

Sweepers are small, schooling fishes that reflect a
coppery or silvery sheen. They inhabit coral reefs in the
tropical Atlantic and Indo-Pacific. Hiding from reef
predators, hundreds hover in caves and under ledges by
day. At night they swirl over the reefs, some species
sweeping the water for tiny plankton. Glassy sweepers,
Pempheris schomburgki, are among the largest, and
exhibit the large eyes helpful for seeing in dimly
lit water.

Archerfishes

family Toxotidae   order Perciformes

Insects crawling on plants bordering mangrove swamps
and estuaries fall prey to sharp-shooting archerfishes,
which can also knock hovering insects out of the air with
rapidly fired drops of water.

An archerfish moves to the surface to take aim. It
squeezes its gills to force water through its mouth. Like a
bullet fired through a rifle barrel, the water travels
through a tube formed by the archerfish's tongue
pressed against a groove in its mouth.

Archerfish rarely miss, being accurate at distances of
up to three feet. With practice, they can hit objects as far
away as 10 feet. Besides shooting down insects, archerfish leap to catch prey, or eat surface-swimming animals.

Spotfin archerfish *Toxotes chatareus*

In the Aquarium, archerfish feed by shooting at pieces of fish and meat placed on a target. Older fish train newcomers. In the wild, young archerfish learn by the time they are half-grown.

Archerfish reach lengths of 10 inches. They linger at the surfaces of rivers, brackish estuaries and coastal waters of Asia, Africa and Australia. All archerfish belong to the genus *Toxotes,* which means "bow-man."

Sea Chubs

family Kyphosidae   order Perciformes

Bermuda chubs, *Kyphosus sectatrix,* reach lengths of 30 inches. At this size they are exciting game fish. Besides a largely vegetarian diet, chubs will consume any tiny animals associated with algae.

The common Bermuda chub belongs to a family of tropical and temperate marine fishes known as rudderfishes and nibblers. The former describes the behavior of those that follow beneath ships. When young, they hover beneath flotsam and clumps of sargassum weed. Nibbler refers to the opaleyes, *Girella nigricans,* that continually pick at and nibble on algae and, in close confinement, each other. It is a common tidepool and shallow-water species of the California coast.

Bermuda chubs *Kyphosus sectatrix*

Spadefishes, Batfishes

family Ephippidae   order Perciformes

Batfishes and spadefishes rely on dark colors and mimicry to survive in their tropical ocean environments.

   The Indo-Pacific batfish, *Platax pinnatus,* is jet black, its tall, graceful fins boldly edged in orange. These are the same colors displayed by several toxic nudibranchs and flatworms, which the juvenile fish further resembles when it swims on its side, fluttering its fins.

Juvenile pinnatus batfish
Platax pinnatus

School of Atlantic spadefish
Chaetodipterus faber

Young spadefish mimic mangrove pods or floating leaves by drifting on their sides at the surface, heads tilted downward. When alarmed, some species stop swimming upright and sink to the bottom, pretending to be dead leaves.

   Silvery, dark-banded Atlantic spadefish, *Chaetodipterus faber,* grow to be quite large, over three feet long. Schools cruise the shallows and reefs feeding on shellfish, sponges, worms, gorgonians and algae. They range from Cape Cod to Brazil.

Scat
Scatophagus argus

Scats

family Scatophagidae   order Perciformes

Tropical aquarium hobbyists enjoy the lively natures of
these fish, imported from coastal waters and estuaries in
the Indo-Pacific. As they grow, young common scats,
Scatophagus argus, lose their orange blush, leaving only
the dark spots characteristic of adults.

In the wild, scats feed on bottom debris and
vegetation. Their abundance near sewer outfalls
contributes to an unsavory reputation as trash feeders.
(*Scatophagus* means "dung-eater.")

Butterflyfishes

family Chaetodontidae   order Perciformes

Pairs of brilliant butterflyfish flit from coral head to
coral head, one dashing to catch up with the other in the
manner of their winged, fluttering namesakes.

Bright patterns and colors serve to identify each
species to other butterflyfish, warn other animals that a
territory is being defended or camouflage the fish from
predators unable to see it against the riotous seascape of
a tropical reef. Most butterflyfish are small, from four to
six inches. (The larger angelfishes were once grouped
with butterflyfishes, but are placed in their own family
because of the spines on their gill covers.)

Coral gardens throughout the world host the many
varieties of these colorful fishes. As though moving from
flower to flower, butterflyfish roam the reef, picking and
probing in search of tiny shrimps, crabs, worms, living
coral animals and algae. Bristly teeth line their small
mouths, which are well adapted for reaching into and
scraping reef crevices (*chaetodon* means "bristle tooth").

Four-spot butterflyfish
Chaetodon quadrimaculatus

Pebbled butterflyfish
Chaetodon multicinctus

Pennant butterflyfish
Heniochus acuminatus

Delicate long snouts ending in small mouths aid several species in probing deep into nooks and crannies for the hidden food others cannot reach. The most extreme belongs to the Pacific longnose butterflyfish, *Forcipiger longisrostris,* its snout even longer than the prominent feature displayed by the more abundant longsnout butterfly, *Forcipiger flavissimus.* Similarly, a deep-water, Caribbean longsnout butterflyfish, *Chaetodon aculeatus,* relies on its narrow proboscis to retrieve small invertebrates from between the spines of sea urchins and from the tentacles of tubeworms. Longnosed species on exhibit nibble at "fishburger" that aquarists pack into the corals in order to get these finicky fishes to eat.

The faces and eyes of some butterflyfish are masked with dark bands. At the other end, near the tail, glaring eye spots may fool predators into lunging for the wrong

end. The reef butterflyfish, *Chaetodon sedentarius,*
illustrates such protective coloring. It is one of the most
common in the West Indian part of its Atlantic range
that extends from Massachusetts to the Gulf of Mexico.

Butterflyfishes also protect themselves with sharp
prominent dorsal spines used as jabbing weapons when
held erect. Belligerent species, like the fiesty, longnosed
copper banded butterfly, *Chelmon rostratus,* even inflict
wounds on their own kind.

Butterflyfishes disappear from the reef scene at night
when larger sea animals move in to feed. Easily slipping
their pancake-thin bodies into reef crevices, butterflyfish
rest until daylight. Some fade and change into drabber
colors at night as further protection.

Many beautiful, lively species are known and
exhibited in the saltwater galleries.

Orange-tailed butterflyfish
Chaetodon xanthurus

Longsnout butterflyfish
Forcipiger flavissimus

A red tail marks the six-inch collared butterflyfish, *Chaetodon collare,* from the Philippines.

Orange-tailed butterflyfish, *Chaetodon xanthurus,* are popular aquarium animals imported from the Philippines.

The pebbled butterflyfish, *Chaetodon multicinctus,* is known only from the Hawaiian islands where it feeds on *Porites* and *Pocillopora* corals, algae, polychaete worms and small shrimps.

A swath of blue stains the yellow flanks of the blue-back butterflyfish, *Chaetodon plebeius,* a species widespread in the Great Barrier Reef.

A mask darkens the face of the raccoon butterflyfish, *Chaetodon lunula,* of the Indo-Pacific.

Exotic black and white pennant butterflyfish, *Heniochus,* waft a streaming banner, really the fourth dorsal spine that arches over the back and beyond the tail.

Threadfin butterflyfish, *Chaetodon auriga,* feature a slender extension of the last spine of the dorsal fin.

Angelfishes

family Pomacanthidae   order Perciformes

"Angels of the reefs," named for the angelic profile of their nearly continuous fins, are conspicuous inhabitants of tropical seas. Angelfish rarely move deeper than 50 feet, and usually swim alone or in pairs. Inquisitive animals, they traverse their reefs in search of algae, sponges, gorgonians, tunicates, hydroids or zoanthids.

Curious angelfish sometimes approach divers who enjoy rewarding such boldness with scraps of food. During the daily feedings in the Coral Reef Exhibit, the diver is usually welcomed by eager angelfishes crowding around the dive mask or bucket of food.

Angelfishes have small, bristly teeth like those of the closely related butterflyfishes. Compared to the butterflyfishes, however, angelfishes are considerably larger and flaunt sharp cheek spines. Young angelfishes differ dramatically from adults in both color and pattern, usually displaying bright yellow or white stripes on black to advertise their cleaning behavior. Many also "flutter-swim" as a further signal to other species that their cleaning station is open for service. Most juveniles, unlike their more tolerant parents, stay near one crevice and fiercely defend it, only allowing clients to approach. Older fish are not cleaners.

Close-up of cheek spine on a princess angelfish, *Holacanthus passer*

The most dramatic color change from young to adult occurs as the Pacific emperor angelfish, *Pomacanthus imperator,* matures. Concentric white circles disrupt the young's dark blue body. Adults are brilliant blue and yellow.

One of the most common Atlantic angelfish is the shy, secretive rock beauty, *Holacanthus tricolor.* Retreating into crevices when startled, it never ventures far from home.

The queen angelfish, *Holacanthus ciliaris,* not surprisingly called the most beautiful fish in the world, has few rivals. Twelve inches of electric blues and yellows are capped by a blue and black crown. The blue angelfish, *Holacanthus bermudensis,* looks like a pale version of its regal cousin. The young of each are nearly identical. The two species often hybridize.

Blue angelfish
Holacanthus bermudensis

Queen angelfish
Holacanthus ciliaris

French and grey angelfishes are also nearly identical as juveniles, but adults only share the thin, pancake shape and do not crossbreed. The striking French angelfish can be distinguished by a gold spot near each cheek and a gold edge on each black scale. At one foot in length, it is only half the size of its more subtly colored grey relative.

Adult French angelfish
Pomacanthus paru

Adult grey angelfish
Pomacanthus arcuatus

The juvenile grey angelfish, *Pomacanthus arcuatus,* has vivid yellow stripes.

Pygmy species rarely exceed 10 inches and often inhabit deeper water. However, pretty lemonpeels, *Centropyge flavissimus,* inhabit shallow, sheltered lagoons in the Pacific where they graze on algae.

Deeper-water pygmies include the russet and blue Potter's angelfish, *Centropyge potteri,* named for the

Lemonpeel
Centropyge flavissimus

first director of the Waikiki Aquarium in Hawaii. Its range is limited to the Hawaiian Islands.

Striking blue and yellow pygmies, *Centropyge bicolor,* are also only found below depths of 33 feet.

The prized flame angelfish, *Centropyge loriculus,* adds a brilliance to displays with its red and yellow hues. It matures at a mere four inches in length.

Because of their small size, fiesty natures and lollipop colors, pygmies are favorite exhibit animals.

Leaffishes

family Nandidae   order Perciformes

A leaf lazily drifting in the current suddenly engulfs a fish nearly half its size. The remarkable leaffish strikes again, appeasing its voracious appetite through stealth and mimicry. In rivers in Asia, South America and Africa, mottled brown-green leaffishes float among dead leaves, heads downward, their chin barbels resembling broken stems. Extendible mouths shoot out to snap up other fish with lightning speed.

Juvenile African leaffish
Polycentropsis abbreviata

Mimicry protects as well, but when startled, these fish will leap out of the water as high as eight inches.

Popular aquarium species include the four-inch South American leaffish, *Monocirrhus polyacanthus,* and the Asian species, *Nandus nandus,* twice as large. The African species is *Polycentropsis abbreviata,* which grows to only three inches.

Black surfperch
Embiotoca jacksoni

Surfperches

family Embiotocidae   order Perciformes

Just beyond the breaking waves of the Pacific surf zone
are found fishes noted for giving birth to live young.
Female surfperches produce broods of 8 to 36 young, and
have reproduced in Aquarium exhibit tanks.

Surfperches are most abundant off the coast of
California, and several are important commercially, in
particular, the white seaperch, *Phanerodon furcatus.*
Sport fishermen also cast for the shiner seaperch,
Cymatogaster aggregata, abundant in harbors and
around wharves in San Francisco Bay. The sea chub,
Ditrema temmincki, delights Japanese seafood
gourmets. The rubberlip seaperch, *Rhacochilus toxotes,*
is one of the largest of this family at 18 inches.

Cichlids

family Cichlidae   order Perciformes

It is possible to display only a sampling of the hundreds
of species in this large family. Cichlids (sick-lids) are a
diverse group. The bewildering variety of forms and
habits allow them to take advantage of almost every
kind of freshwater habitat. Most prefer still water with
plenty of shelter nearby. They range in size from one-
and-one-half inches to the thirty-inch South American
food fish, the tucunare, *Cichla ocellaris.*

Cichlids live in the warm lakes and rivers of the
southwestern United States, Central and South
America, Africa and the coastal waters of India. The Rio
Grande cichlid, *Cichlasoma cyanoguttatum,* is the only
cichlid native to the United States. In many ways,
cichlids are tropical versions of the cooler water
sunfishes and basses.

Three species of tucunares, *Cichla* sp., collected in Venezuela in 1982.

Tucunare, *Cichla ocellaris,* with gills flared.

In the African Great Lakes, many cichlids have become so adapted to their isolated, stable environments that they are unlike any others. A community display in Gallery 6 teems with various representatives, including zebra cichlids, *Pseudotropheus zebra,* and yellow cichlids, *Labeotropheus tropheus.*

Cichlids feed in almost every way imaginable. Different species will either scrape algae from rocks, strain plankton, crush shellfish and snails, sift mud and sand for insect larvae or eat other fish. Earth-eaters, *Geophagus,* gobble mouthfuls of gravel and scrape off any edible material before spitting out the debris. Some cichlids even specialize in eating fish eyes as part of their diet. The eight-inch Malawi eye-biter, *Haplochromis compressiceps,* has hooked teeth that rip eyes out instantly. Even more exotic is the diet of the scale-eaters, which includes scales scraped from the skin of sluggish bottom-dwellers.

Cichlids breed readily and grow quickly, enhancing their attraction to aquarists who appreciate their diverse habits and often bright colors. Males are more brilliantly colored than females. Conspicuous colors help cichlids recognize their own kind in the often dense communities in which they live. Less colorful species are usually counter-shaded for protection. Darker ones frequent rocky areas while lighter varieties are found close to sandy shores. Silvery cichlids live in open water, and striped ones hide among the plants. Spotted cichlids usually rely on their patterns to confuse predators. Twelve-inch oscars, *Astronotus ocellatus,* are also called peacock-eyed cichlids because of their distinctive orange and black marks.

Breeding habits vary greatly among cichlids. Territorial species spawn in nests guarded by the attentive parents. They angrily shake fins at intruders and attack faces thrust too close to exhibit glass. A few are cannibalistic while others shelter eggs and young in their mouths for safekeeping.

Mouth-brooders include the cherrybelly cichlid, *Pelvicachromis pulcher.* It lives in a wide range of habitats in West Africa, and is known throughout rivers and swamps in forests or savannahs. Fasting males carry the eggs for 11 to 13 days.

Among the Nile mouth-brooders, *Tilapia nilotica,* the female broods the young. This plankton-eating species is

Freshwater angelfish
Pterophyllum scalare

Oscar
Astronotus ocellatus

Ram
Apistogramma sp.

Lyretail African cichlid
Lamprologus brichardi

one of the largest cichlids and is highly valued as food.
Widely distributed across East and West Africa and
along the Nile to Israel, it reaches lengths of nearly 20
inches. Rugged, fast-growing *Tilapia* reach weights of
up to 20 pounds and are pond-cultured as a major food
source throughout Asia and Africa. They thrive even in
polluted waters where they feed on algae and other
aquatic plants and reproduce quickly. Tiger cichlids,
Tilapia mariae, frequently spawn in the Aquarium.

In a display of extreme parental care, the beautiful,
peaceful discus, or pompadorfish, *Symphysodon
aequifasciata,* feeds its young with a slimy mucus
secreted from its skin. Upon hatching, the fry swarm
over the sides of either parent. These delicate fish thrive
only in quiet, heavily planted aquariums that duplicate
their natural habitat among plants and logs in the
backwaters of the Amazon River system.

Discus or pompador fish
Symphysodon aequifasciata

From these waters, collectors also receive the well-
known, graceful, freshwater angelfish, *Pterophyllum
scalare.* Arched fins and dark bands camouflage the six-
inch silvery fish among the weedy areas of rivers.
(It is not related to the tropical reef angelfishes,
Pomacanthidae.)

Also popular are pretty dwarf species such as the
dwarf cichlids, *Apistogramma ramerizi.* Long streamers
trail from their pelvic fins. The fish reach lengths of only
a few inches.

Many larger species are belligerent and are less
desirable as pets. For example, the spotted Jack
Dempsey from South America, *Cichlasoma biocellatus,*

must be kept alone. Because of its pugnacious behavior, this species was named for the one-time world heavyweight boxing champion.

Pretty flag cichlids, *C. festivum,* and banded cichlids, *C. severum,* will meticulously rearrange their tanks while preparing to lay up to 1,000 eggs. A spectacular member of this genus is the firemouth, *C. meeki,* which flaunts a blazing red chest.

Damselfishes

family Pomacentridae   order Perciformes

Garibaldi
Hypsypops rubicundus

Spritely, quarrelsome little damselfishes inhabit tropical coral reefs and rocky coastal regions worldwide. They feed on smaller marine animals and plants, depending upon their speed and agility for survival.

Only the flamboyant garibaldi, *Hypsypops rubicundus,* is found in cooler seas. Bright orange, it is named for the Italian general who wore a bright red shirt. These pugnacious fish and their blue-spotted young frequent the kelp beds off the coast of southern California. Characteristic of damselfishes, the territorial males guard the eggs. Garibaldis lay their eggs on red algae after it has been cultivated into a nest. Damselfishes will vigorously defend their nests and territories against intruders of any size, including divers.

Anemonefishes, *Amphiprion* and *Premnas,* are well known for their death-defying partnerships with fish-eating anemones. Performing an elaborate ballet, the small anemonefish brushes its host's tentacles and dashes away. Gradually the fish exposes more of its body until it can stay among the tentacles without harm. The dance covers the fish with the protective mucus that keeps the anemone from stinging itself. Anemonefish will live only with certain anemones, prefering a specific host. Some move freely from one type to another, resembling bees in a clover field. Others must slowly readjust to each new anemone.

Anemonefish dart out of their havens to snap up plankton and tiny sea animals, or to chase away anemone predators such as butterflyfishes. Some occasionally bring tidbits of food to their hosts and clean debris from the mouth area. In return, the little fish receive protection from larger reef animals that avoid the stinging tentacles.

Anemonefish are sometimes called clown fish because of their vivid orange and white markings. The number and position of white bands vary between species,

and serve to camouflage them among the tentacles of
their hosts.

Pairs of the four-inch anemonefish, *Amphiprion
bicinctus,* from the Red Sea, usually share the same
anemone. They shift their territory as the host slowly
moves across the reef. Groups of about 20 young live
together in the anemone, *Radianthus,* frequently seen
in tidepools.

In the Pacific, the little clown anemonefish,
Amphiprion ocellaris, lays and guards its eggs next to
the carpet anemone, *Stoichactis.*

Hundreds of Pacific humbugs of the genus *Dascyllus*
hover over their chosen coral heads until danger is
sensed, when all will suddenly disappear into previously
claimed crevices. Because they often live in association
with the shallow-water coral, *Stylophora,* their range is
limited in depth. Many of these dark-banded species are

Clown anemonefish
Amphiprion ocellaris

Sergeant major
Abudefduf saxatilis

Brown chromis
*Chromis
multileniata*

imported for aquariums, where they must be kept alone or provided with plenty of hiding places to avoid quarrels.

Yellowtail damsels, *Microspathodon chrysurus,* from the Caribbean, behave similarly. The young seek shelter in fire coral, *Millepora.* Known as jewelfish, the juveniles have metallic-blue spots. The stunning adults sport vivid blue freckles on their dark heads and have bright yellow tails.

The vertical black and gold bands of the fiesty little sergeant majors, *Abudefduf saxatilis,* resemble military chevrons, hence their name. Distributed worldwide in tropical waters, they are often the most conspicuous species of reefs, sand flats or around piers. A more brilliant member of the genus is the yellow-tailed blue Pacific species, *Glyphidodontops cyaneus.*

Many damselfishes are blue, including blue chromis, *Chromis cyaneus.* This species is often found in deeper water over patch reefs where large schools can be seen harvesting the floating plankton fields.

Hawkfishes

family Cirrhitidae   order Perciformes

Hawkfishes are small tropical reef fish sometimes colored brilliant red and noted for the tufts of tissue on their dorsal spines. One Atlantic species, *Amblycirrhitus pinos,* is also the smallest, rarely exceeding three inches. Despite its size, it is just as voracious as its larger relatives.

The longnose hawkfish, *Oxycirrhites typus,* has an exaggerated snout compared to other family members.

Longnose hawkfish
Oxycirrhites typus

It is found only in the East Indies and Hawaii.
Hawkfishes, including the striking, ten-inch hawkfish,
Paracirrhites forsteri, are most numerous and
widespread in the Indo-Pacific.

Hawkfishes are frequently found perched atop a rock
or bit of coral. From here they pounce like a hawk to
snap up a passing shrimp or other morsel. Hawaiians
call them *pilikoa,* "coral-clinging," for they will stay
with the same coral head even when hauled out of water.

Mullets
family Muglidae   order Perciformes

Most mullets sift mouthfuls of mud and sand containing
tiny plants and animals, which pass through their
heavily muscled stomachs and extremely long intestines
(characteristic of vegetarians). They have blunt heads
and thick, inverted-V-shaped lips well suited to such
dining habits and useful in grazing on fine algae.

Striped mullet
Mugil cephalus

Many are valuable food fish throughout their range,
extending from shallow coasts into brackish and fresh
water in tropical regions. The striped mullet, *Mugil
cephalus,* grows to a length of three feet. Its fast growth
rate makes it a desirable fish for brackish and saltwater
pond culture. Commercial fishermen most frequently
catch the white mullet, *Mugil curema,* off the coast
of Florida.

Barracudas
family Sphyraenidae   order Perciformes

Pointed jaws lined with formidable teeth could belong to
no other than the "tiger of the sea," the great barracuda,
Sphyraena barracuda.

These fierce marine predators are feared almost as
much as sharks in Caribbean waters, where records of
over 30 attacks on humans bear witness to their ferocity.
The fact that the attacks occur mostly in cloudy water
implies cases of mistaken identity.

Barracudas locate their food largely by sight,
attacking brightly colored or erratically moving objects.
Splashing swimmers wearing jewelry or white sneakers
catch their attention, as do freshly speared fish. They
are very inquisitive and will follow divers for hours.

Silver, torpedo-slim great barracudas reach lengths of
six feet, though anglers have yet to beat the 1932 world
record of 66 inches and 106 pounds. Their flesh,
considered excellent eating, may concentrate ciguatera

poisons from the grunts, jacks, sea basses and other reef fish they eat.

Lone individuals patrol the coral heads and reefs of all tropical seas as they do in the Coral Reef Exhibit. Their active habits and untamable natures make them difficult to care for in captivity.

Smaller species, such as the two-foot guaguanche, *S. guachancho,* and the northern sennet, *S. borealis,* frequently occur in large schools. Both range from New England to Brazil. The four-foot Pacific species, *S. argentea,* frequents shallow, inshore waters from Alaska to Baja, California, where it is netted or hooked by commercial and sport fishermen.

Barracuda, *Sphyraena barracuda,* with pilotfish.

Threadfins

family Polynemidae   order Perciformes

Threadfins "feel" the sea floor with long streamers extending from their specialized pectoral fins. They probe for crabs, prawns and fishes to satisfy their carnivorous appetites. Found in coastal waters and estuaries of warm seas, most average around 18 inches. The barbu, *Polydactylus approximans,* frequents the sand flats of the Atlantic from New Jersey to Uraguay. Near India, the giant threadfin, *Eleutheronema tetradactylum,* grows to be six feet long, and is commercially valuable.

Wrasses

family Labridae   order Perciformes

Most wrasses are brightly colored tropical reef fish. Particularly abundant on Hawaiian reefs, wrasses are widespread in the Indo-Pacific and tropical Atlantic areas. Diverse in form and color, perhaps the most bizarre is the foot-long bird wrasse, *Gomphosus,* the only species with a long curving snout.

Because wrasses sleep buried in the sand at night, Hawaiians call many of them "lolo," meaning lazy. Evidence of "rapid eye movement" while they doze leads some scientists to wonder if wrasses may even dream.

Sizes vary considerably. The smallest species are the conspicuously striped cleaners, *Labroides,* which rarely exceed three inches. They set up stations on shallow reefs, and vigorously guard them from other wrasses. Jacks, groupers, snappers, parrotfishes and eels, loaded with parasites, stop by for a cleaning.

At the other end of the size scale is the five-foot giant wrasse, *Cheilinus,* from the deeper reef drop-offs in the Indo-Pacific. Older individuals develop large bumps on their foreheads, hence one species name, humpheaded maori.

Carnivorous fishes, most wrasses have powerful jaws armed with strong canine teeth, a feature well illustrated by the vivid harlequin tusk fish, *Lienardella fasciata.* Additional rows of back molars crush snails, clams, crabs and other shellfish.

Harlequin tusk fish
Lienardella fasciata

Bird wrasse
Gomphosus varius

Many other species are equally as brilliantly colored as the orange and purple tusk fish. The twinspot wrasse, *Coris aygula,* from the Indo-Pacific, displays startling patterns. Beautiful hues of green, blue, red, orange and yellow decorate the rainbow wrasse, *Thalassoma lunare,* common in Indo-Pacific tidepools.

Male wrasses often look very different from the females and young. Among the Atlantic blueheads, *Thalassoma bifasciatum,* certain males have blue heads. Called super males, it is thought that these were once females that later became males. Super males mate with females one at a time, unlike other males and females that spawn in schools. The latter remain yellow, lacking the super males' bright blue head.

More subdued in color are the abundant slippery dicks, *Halichoeres bivittatus,* frequently the most common wrasse in shallow tropical waters. These small, nine-inch fish are everywhere, feeding on sea urchins, crabs

Twinspot wrasse
Coris aygula

Tautog
Tautoga onitis

Bicolor hogfish
Bodianus axillaris

Slippery dick
Halichoeres bivittatus

and brittle stars and being eaten by many larger fishes. A two-foot relative, the pudding wife, *Halichoeres radiatus,* is much less commonly encountered in the Caribbean.

The tautog, *Tautoga onitis,* is an Atlantic species that grows to lengths of three feet. Abundant on rocky shores, it lurks behind rocks until a tempting crab or lobster prompts a quick lunge.

The smaller Atlantic cunner, or sea perch, *Tautogolabrus adspersus,* schools in shallows near wharves and piers.

West Indians favor the pretty hogfish, *Lachnolaimus maximus,* for its fine flavor. Named for the porcine appearance of its snout, its long spines and frequent color changes make it a striking display fish, as is the beautiful Spanish hogfish, *Bodianus rufus.*

The senorita, *Oxyjulis californica,* is found in kelp beds lining the coasts of California and Mexico.

Parrotfishes

family Scaridae   order Perciformes

Colorful parrotfishes scrape algae from corals, and may bite off chunks of the tropical reefs with their beak-like teeth. Molars far back in their throats can crush the hard, indigestible coral skeleton into fine sand.

No less beautiful than their avian namesakes, parrotfishes exhibit many different, often confusing colors. Individuals may instantly blend in with changing backgrounds. Also, many males and females differ so greatly that biologists have difficulty distinguishing the same species. The young frequently display their own unique stripes.

Juvenile bicolor parrotfish
Cetoscarus bicolor

Parrotfishes may also change sex. Females that become males are called super males, and are distinctly marked with patterns that differ from those of normal males.

Parrotfishes graze on reefs during the day, their behavior earning the nickname "cattle of the sea." At night, some wedge into crevices, while others, such as the blue parrotfish, *Scarus coeruleus,* spend half an hour spinning a mucous cocoon. Few nocturnal reef predators will bother with the gooey mess.

Blue parrotfishes are a common species in the Caribbean. They reach lengths of four feet, the largest individuals occurring in deeper water. Older males often develop very noticeable bumps on their foreheads.

Smaller species seldom exceed 18 inches, including the Caribbean redfin parrotfish, *Sparisoma rubripinne.* Many of these smaller parrotfishes only graze on algae and cause little damage to corals.

Blue parrot
Scarus coeruleus

Parrotfish sleeping in a cocoon.

Jawfishes

family Opistognathidae   order Perciformes

These little marine "engineers" excavate burrows in the
sandy floor of most tropical seas. Jawfishes constantly
tend their foot-long tunnels, fastidiously cleaning and
enlarging them as they grow. Small fishes, most are
mature at four to six inches. In their scoopshovel mouths
they haul rock, coral rubble and bits of shell used as rip-
rap to prevent the entrance from caving in. At the first
sign of danger they disappear into their chambers, often
tail first.

Jawfishes vigorously guard their burrows and
surrounding territory, skirmishing with any neighbors
bold enough to ignore boundary lines. A few mouthfuls
of debris dumped into a rival's burrow keeps the offender
busily cleaning. An angry jawfish may rush at another,
gills flaring, fins held out and enormous mouth agape.

Usually content to hover just above their custom-built
"condos," jawfish rarely venture far, even when
pursuing a meal of tiny brine shrimp. "Tail-standers,"
they swim nearly vertically with the aid of pectoral and
tail fins.

The pale and delicate hues of the yellowhead jawfish,
Opistognathus aurifrons, blend in with white coral
sands. Other species are mottled or brownish in color,
their large blue-green eyes located above prominent,
scowling jaws.

Yellowhead jawfish *Opistognathus aurofrons*

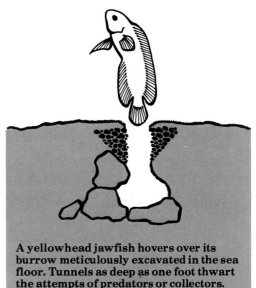

A yellowhead jawfish hovers over its
burrow meticulously excavated in the sea
floor. Tunnels as deep as one foot thwart
the attempts of predators or collectors.

Eel Blennies

family Congrogadidae   order Perciformes

Secretive eel blennies hide among rocks, or burrow in sand and mud. Their long, skinny bodies are edged with fins that often merge with the tail.

Emerald eel blennies, *Congrogadus subducens,* are named for their mottled green patterns. They are frequently found with their fifteen-inch bodies tucked into rocky crannies in Pacific tidepools.

Emerald eel blennies
Congrogadus subducens

Island kelpfish
Alloclinus holderi

Clinids, Hairy blennies

family Clinidae   order Perciformes

This diverse family is well represented in tropical seas and the southern hemisphere. Often confused with blennies, clinids can be distinguished by the presence of scales (blennies are scaleless). To add to the confusion, a number of clinids are named blenny.

Many clinids present a comical image, their blunt heads capped by fringes of tentacles. Growths over the eyes and on the back of the neck give rise to the name hairy blenny. Typical of the hairy blennies is the eight-inch *Labrisomus nuchipinnis,* a familiar inhabitant of ankle-deep water in the Caribbean.

Most live on or near the bottom in a variety of adopted dwellings. Several tiny species such as the one-and-one-half-inch eelgrass blenny, *Stathmonotus stahli,* live in the hundreds of canals riddling large sponges. These little green fish also inhabit crevices in *Porites* corals.

Another Caribbean sponge-dweller is the checkered blenny, *Starksia ocellata,* capable of altering its dull brown phase to live up to its name.

Extremely territorial, bluethroat pikeblennies, *Chaenopsis ocellata,* prefer to live alone in old worm tubes in seagrass beds, and will drive off any unwelcome visitors. Males dash at intruders with mouths wide open, flashing blue throats and gill covers. Dusky brown females lack this war paint as well as the orange spot near the dorsal fin.

Males also steal the show among the rosy blennies, *Malacoctenus macropus,* one of the most common of the Atlantic clinids. It is a small fish, only two and one-half inches long.

The largest clinid is the two-foot giant kelpfish, *Heterostichus rostratus,* a species notorious for changing colors to match its Pacific coast habitat.

Threefin blennies, family Tripterygiidae, closely resemble the clinids and include the miniature *Tripterygion nanus.* Females are fully mature when only three-quarters of an inch long.

Blenny
Entomacrodus sp.

Blennies

family Blenniidae   order Perciformes

Blennies are small, active fishes living among the rocks and seaweed on almost every suitable shore. Many are prettily marked, but with dark colors that blend in with the rockweed in which they hide. None has scales.

Fringy tufts above their eyes and on their blunt foreheads give many a comical and unmistakable appearance. Bright red lips further distinguish a typical species, the redlip blenny, *Ophioblennius atlanticus.*

Five-inch adults are abundant bottom-dwellers near reefs and rocky shores. Redlip blennies range from North Carolina and Bermuda through the Caribbean and Gulf of Mexico.

Like other blennies, males guard the eggs laid in crevices. The young spend some time living in the open ocean before settling down to life on the rocks.

Blennies choose unusual places to live: in the dead shells of oysters, cast-off crockery, beer cans, under rocks or in caves, to name a few.

In the rocky tidepools of the Indo-Pacific, the agile rock skipper or hopper, *Alticops periophthalmus,* jumps and skips over rocks in search of food.

Blennies have teeth of varying size; they are also called combtooth blennies. Most blennies feed on small invertebrates and worms, some biting off the feet of barnacles that protrude from shells to sweep the water. The Atlantic pearl blenny, *Entomacrodus nigricans,* feeds largely on algae. In some species, long, curving teeth extend from the lower jaw.

Several blennies are masters of mimicry and use their teeth to attack larger fishes that have been fooled by their costume and behavior. One such blenny, *Aspidontus taeniatus,* resembles the harmless cleaner wrasse, *Labroides dimidiatus,* complete with a dark stripe on its bright blue body. Fish, approaching to be cleaned of parasites, are instead ambushed by the mimic blenny, which nips out pieces of skin or gill.

One Red Sea species inflicts venomous bites with its large fangs. Predators usually avoid the three-inch *Meiacanthus nigrolineatus.* The mimic blenny, *Plagiotremus townsendi,* wearing matching colors and, pretending to be the venomous species, boldly swims up to larger fish. It quickly bites off mouthfuls of skin and scales.

While most blennies are only two or three inches long, the largest, the hair-tailed blenny, *Xiphasia setifer,* measures nearly two feet, and is feared by Pacific pearl divers.

Gunnels

family Pholidae   order Perciformes

Left stranded by low tides, gunnels will nestle into seaweed to stay moist until the surf returns. These secretive fishes frequent the rocky coasts and tide pools of cold oceans.

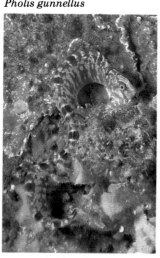

Rock gunnel
Pholis gunnellus

Long, skinny gunnels normally hide under rocks and in crevices. The rock gunnel, *Pholis gunnellus,* lays its eggs there, then curls around the clump to guard it until the fry hatch a month later. The adults of this common North Atlantic species reach lengths of ten inches. Many carry a form of parasitic worm on their skins, which infests the sea birds that feed heavily on them.

On the Pacific coast, some of the better known forms are the colorful red and green rockweed gunnel, *Xererpes fucorum,* and the crescent gunnel, *Pholis laeta.* The latter is characterized by a series of black, crescent-shaped markings along the base of the dorsal fin, which enclose yellow or orange areas. Both species grow to ten inches.

Wolfishes, Wolf-eels

family Anarhichadidae   order Perciformes

Deep-water wolfishes and wolf-eels are well known for their heavy-duty canine teeth. Less visible, the back, crushing molars make easy work of crab, mollusc or sea urchin shells.

Wolfishes, *Anarhicas,* live to 900 feet deep in the Atlantic, where the spotted species grows to lengths of over six feet. In Europe, where they are known as catfishes, commercial fishermen bring them up in trawls.

In the Pacific, territorial wolf-eels, *Anarrhichthys ocellatus,* stake out rocky abodes on the sea floor. They occur from the shallows to considerable depths. Parents take turns curling themselves around clumps of thousands of eggs, protecting them until they hatch. Baby wolf-eels were successfully raised for the first time at the Vancouver Aquarium in 1978.

Wolf-eel
Anarrhichthys ocellatus

Sand Lances

family Ammodytidae   order Perciformes

Sand lances are small, silvery, plankton-eating fishes.
They live in the surf zones of arctic, cool and warm seas.
These timid fish burrow into the sand in shallow water
to escape the hoards of animals that feed on them —
cods, herrings, mackerels, sea birds and dolphins.

When buried, they are often left high and dry by the
receding tide. A person stamping on the sand will
frequently be surprised to see a number of sand lances
pop out of the beach nearby.

The eight-inch American sand lance, *Ammodytes
americanus,* ranges from Labrador to Cape Hatteras.
Like many other species of this family, its attenuated,
silvery body is counter-shaded with metallic blue green
on top and white below.

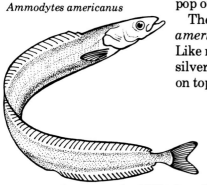

Sand lance
Ammodytes americanus

Yellowhead sleeper goby
Eleotroides strigatus

Sleeper Gobies

family Eleotridae   order Perciformes

These large tropical fishes lie still among the weeds for
long periods and move only when disturbed, hence the
name "sleepers." Although sometimes called gobies,
sleepers do not have the goby trademark of a suction
disc formed by fused bottom fins.

The Atlantic fat sleeper, *Dormitator maculatus,* lies in
the mud of intertidal areas, brackish pools and river
mouths from North Carolina to the Gulf of Mexico.

Other sleepers that are more active sometimes school
over coral reefs, but always near hiding places. Some,
Vireosa, for example, even seek shelter in the living
giant clam, *Tridacna,* or large rock oysters. Startled by
the little fish ducking inside, the shells usually close but
leave the sleeper unharmed.

Largest of the group are two-foot-long sleepers known
as bigmouth sleepers or "guavinas," *Gobiomorus
dormitor,* which inhabit the waters of Central America.

Gobies
family Gobiidae   order Perciformes

Gobies are small, colorful fishes making up many of the species that inhabit the shallow coastal waters of temperate and tropical seas. They are also found in brackish and fresh water. Most hide in crevices or on the bottom, while some burrow in the mud or spend long periods on land. Strange partnerships exist between a number of gobies and other mud-dwelling sea creatures.

Although diverse in habit, most gobies look similar, each possessing a long body, big head and large mouth.

Mudskipper
Periophthalmus barbarus

Neon goby
Gobiosoma oceanops

Firefish
Nemateleotris magnificus

Gobies often have a sucking disc on their undersides formed by the two pelvic fins fused together. With it they cling to rocks in the surge zones and tidal areas.

The tiniest known fish (and vertebrate animal), is a goby, the half-inch-long *Pandaka pygmaea* from the fresh waters of the Philippines. This species and many other freshwater gobies return to the sea to spawn. Indonesian fishermen gather at the rivers to intercept the huge swarms of fry returning to the rivers of their parents. Although small, the young are valued when fried or made into a paste.

Inch-long, sponge-dwelling gobies exhibit features well adapted to their unique homes. Toothed scales on the lower part of the tail of the sponge goby, *Evermannichthys spongicola,* help it crawl through tunnels. The tusked goby, *Risor ruber,* uses its curved "tusks" to tear open sponge walls for a meal of cohabitating invertebrates. Both species are found in large Caribbean sponges such as loggerheads, *Spheciospongia.*

Other abodes include the holes in California mudflats that arrow gobies, *Clevelandia ios,* share with pea crabs or worms. These two-inch fish search estuaries and bays for food until alarmed, when they head into the burrow for shelter. They may also lie in wait and dart out to capture passing plankton. No problem with biting off more than it can chew, the hungry fish simply carries a large piece of food over to a crab to eat and picks up leftovers of a more suitable size.

Acting as sentinels, pairs of gobies of the genus *Smilogobius* stand watch at the entrance to the burrow of their symbiotic host, a snapping shrimp. At the first sign of danger, they dart inside.

The blind goby, *Typhlogobius californiensis,* also shares a burrow with a roommate, but will die if its caretaker, a ghost shrimp, leaves. Sighted at birth, blind gobies soon lose their sight and body color, and never venture from the gravelly hole.

Brilliant members of the family include the neon goby, *Gobiosoma oceanops,* a well-known parasite cleaner of larger reef fish. Customers line up at cleaning stations atop coral heads, waiting for the little goby to rid them of pests. Neons slide over the larger fish, keeping a firm hold with their suction discs.

Even more vivid are the electric reds of the blue-banded goby, *Lythrypnus dalli,* common in crevices below 20 feet off the coast of California. They make dazzling display animals, as do the popular yellow-and-

brown-banded bumblebee gobies, *Brachygobius,* from
brackish waters in Southeast Asia.

The well-named firefish or spike-finned goby,
Nemateleotris magnificus, hovers nearly upright, its
long spike held out in full view. This vibrant fish thrives
amidst the colorful reefs of Micronesia.

In sharp contrast with their spectacular reef-dwelling
relatives, large, drab-colored mudskippers frequent the
tropical tidepools and mangrove swamps of the Indo-
Pacific and West Africa. Left exposed at high tide, these
six-inch acrobats walk, hop or wriggle over rocks, mud
flats and mangrove roots on their strong pectoral fins.
Bulging eyes peer from atop the head. When danger is
seen, the startled fish quickly springs away in bounding
leaps, covering three feet at a shot. Also called
mudspringer, *Periophthalmus barbarus* survives long
periods out of water by gulping air into a spongy cavity
near its gills.

Yellow surgeonfish,
Zebrasoma flavescens,
and close-up of tail spine.

Surgeonfishes, Tangs
family Acanthuridae   order Perciformes

Surgeonfishes carry one or several scalpel-sharp spines
on either side of their tails. These help defend against
predators while they graze, head down, among tropical
reefs. Sideways "slaps" will inflict serious damage to
other fish. Many species sheath their movable weapons
in grooves when resting, while a few carry them fixed
and ready at all times. Bright colors occasionally
surround and highlight the spines.

Surgeonfishes, or tangs (meaning "sharp thorn"),
have hard beaks that scrape algae from rocks and

corals. Evidence of this feeding activity can be seen on the walls of their exhibit tanks. Bristle-toothed surgeonfishes or koles (co-lees), *Ctenochaetus,* have more flexible, tiny teeth for picking very small algae from the bottom.

These pancake-thin and colorful reef-dwellers reach lengths of eight to twelve inches. Colors vary in some individuals and between young fish and adults. The striking blue tang, *Acanthurus coeruleus,* for example, is yellow when young, only later acquiring the deep blue body dramatically outlined in white. One of the Atlantic species, it ranges from New York and Bermuda to Brazil and throughout the West Indies. The longer-snouted yellow surgeonfish, *Zebrasoma flavescens,* is sunny yellow in its Hawaiian range, where it is called *La'ipala,* "yellow leaf."

One of the most common and widely distributed species is the convict tang, or five-banded surgeonfish, *Acanthurus triostegus,* known throughout the tropical Pacific.

Many tangs are considered fine eating, including the largest Atlantic species, the ocean surgeon, *Acanthurus bahainus.* However, as with many reef fish, some have been involved in cases of food poisoning.

The well-developed horn adorning the forehead of the Pacific unicornfish, *Naso brevirostris,* serves no known

Moorish idol
Zanclus canescens

purpose. Young fish have a slight bump that grows as they mature. Unable to get close enough to graze on algae from rocks, unicornfishes feed on the leafier seaweeds at the base of corals.

Sailfin tangs in the genus *Zebrasoma* have extremely large fins covering more area than their bodies. They are commonly found in deeper water near reef edges.

The splendid moorish idol, *Zanclus canescens,* is classified in a separate family, Zanclidae, but is very closely related to the tangs. Its long, arching fin and stunning stripes bring to mind the banner butterflyfish, *Heniochus.* Young moorish idols have a sharp spike at each corner of their distinctive, tube-like snouts. These disappear as the fish grow. Adults develop horny growths on their brows.

Rabbitfishes

family Siganidae   order Perciformes

In weedy, tropical bays and shallow reefs, rabbitfishes nibble and scrape algae off the rocks with "buck" teeth. They are named for their distinctive mouths. Also known as "spinefeet," they have sharp strong spines in their fins that inflict painful wounds. Grooves in the spines may carry venom.

Rabbitfishes are well known for rapidly changing colors, making them difficult to identify. However, unmistakable patches of orange and yellow mark the black-masked foxface, *Lo vulpinus.* Its long snout further sets it apart from other rabbitfishes.

Twinbar rabbitfish, *Siganus virgatus,* in normal colors, and frightened, below.

Labyrinth Fishes

The labyrinth fishes possess curious structures above their gills for storing air. Intricate and many-folded, these organs resemble a maze or labyrinth. Their ability to breathe air allows these Asian and African fishes to survive in weedy, tropical pools and ditches low in oxygen or to withstand drought. Because their gills are inefficient, many would drown if unable to get to the surface.

Most labyrinth fishes are bubble-nest builders. The nest, which floats on the surface, is held together by sticky mucus covering each bubble. It is continually rebuilt as the bubbles burst. Eggs are deposited among the bubbles and when the young hatch, they have ready access to the atmosphere. Those that stray too far from their bubble haven are retrieved by the parents.

Climbing Perches
family Anabantidae   order Perciformes

In 1791, the Danish naturalist Daldorf found a climbing perch, *Anabas,* five feet up the trunk of a palm tree, bathing in rainwater. While seldom found in trees, these Asian and African walking fishes are known to walk about, usually at night, presumably in search of water when their own stagnant pools dry up. They breathe air whether in or out of water, and wobble across land on their rigid gill covers, helped along by their tails at speeds of up to ten feet per minute. Popular food fish, these hardy, ten-inch fish survive for long periods in the marketplace.

Smaller African species, *Ctenopoma,* are frequently imported as aquarium animals although none is particularly colorful.

Siamese Fighting Fish, Paradisefish, Pearl Gouramis
family Belontiidae   order Perciformes

Undoubtedly the most popular of the labyrinth fishes is the Siamese fighting fish, *Betta splendens.* This gorgeous fish was introduced throughout Asia from Siam (now Thailand), where for centuries it has been bred as a fighter. It occurs naturally in stagnant swamps and ditches where it feeds voraciously on mosquito larvae.

Wild specimens are a warm brown or green. Domestic varieties are overlaid with striking patterns of brilliant

Male Siamese fighting fish
Betta splendens

Paradisefish
Macropodus opercularis

blues, greens, reds or black. Exciting pets, many of the
little two-and-one-half-inch fish have been imported for
the hobbyist trade. American breeders have developed
many exotic varieties with enormously enlarged fins,
such as the veiltail fighting fish.

Only the pugnacious territorial males develop the
long, wavy fins and bright colors. They are bred as
champion fighters in Asia. They attack each other on
sight, ripping fins and tearing out scales in staged
contests where huge sums of money are at stake.

A male will also harass a female except when
breeding, when he will carefully construct and tend a
bubble nest. He spits the eggs laid by the female into the
nest, then stays near until the young hatch and can fend
for themselves.

The beautiful paradisefish, *Macropodus opercularis,*
was one of the first tropical aquarium fish imported into
Europe. This long-finned species from the rice paddies of
Southeast Asia has been cultivated for centuries because
of its hardy nature and because it reproduces readily in

captivity. Feisty and pugnacious, they do best when kept isolated.

From weed-choked waterways in Burma come other pretty aquarium species including the thick-lipped gourami, *Colisa labiosa*. It measures a mere three inches long. Even tinier is the two-inch dwarf gourami, *Colisa lalia*. Males of both species display bright red fins.

The long, trailing pelvic fins of the pearl and moonlight gouramis, *Trichogaster,* are typical of the peaceful gouramis that delight home aquarists. The croaking gourami, *Trichopsis vittatus,* serenades its keepers with a high-pitched song each time it gulps air at the surface, the sound possibly amplified by its labyrinth organs.

Pearl gourami
Trichogaster leeri

Kissing gourami
Helostoma temmincki

Kissing Gouramis
family Helostomatidae   order Perciformes

Puckering kissing gouramis, *Helostoma temmincki,* face each other and press their thick lips together. What may really be a threat display has long been mistaken for a display of affection.

Hobbyists enjoy keeping kissing gouramis as pets, but in their native range in Asia, these foot-long fish are caught and eaten.

Giant gourami
Osphronemus goramy

Giant Gourami

family Osphronemidae   order Perciformes

Dwarfing its pretty relatives, the true gourami,
Osphronemus goramy, grows to two feet in length. It
has been introduced far beyond its native range in the
East Indies because of its value as a food source.
Throughout Asia, it is caught in weedy streams and
swamps or raised in ponds and marketed fresh.

Snakeheads

family Channidae   order Perciformes

Snakeheads, named for their broad, heavily scaled
serpentine faces, hungrily feed on other tropical river
animals — frogs, fishes, snakes and insects. These
aggressive predators are able to thrive in stagnant fresh
waters in Asia and Africa by breathing air at the
surface. During periods of drought, snakeheads travel
over land in search of water, or burrow in the mud.

Surviving for several days out of water, these tasty fish are sold in the marketplaces. They range in size from six inches to more than three feet. The largest species is the Southeast Asian red-lined snakefish, *Ophicephalus micropeltes*. Juvenile specimens often appear in aquariums.

Snakehead
Ophicephalus sp.

Zebra spiny eel,
Mastacembelus zebrinus,
buried up to its snout.

Spiny Eels

family Mastacembelidae   order Perciformes

During the day, spiny eels burrow in mud or sand with just their snouts exposed. The most exaggerated snout belongs to the elephant-nosed spiny eel, *Macrognathus aculeatus*.

From their hiding places on the bottom or among the weeds of tropical estuaries and rivers, spiny eels ambush prey. At night they become more active and hunt for insects, small fishes and crustaceans.

Many breathe air and withstand long, dry periods or stagnant, foul water. The larger species exceed lengths of three feet. These are caught as food throughout their range in Asia and Africa. However, their backs are well armed with many erectible, sharp spines that can inflict painful stab wounds on careless fishermen.

Most spiny eels average 15 inches or less and make interesting, if secretive, aquarium animals.

Flatfishes

Pebbles on the bottom suddenly blink and disappear in a flurry of sand as a flatfish pursues a fish, squid or shrimp. Flatfishes usually lie buried up to their bulging, pebble-like eyes. They stay hidden from predators while watching for unsuspecting meals to move within range. This group of curious-looking fishes includes many favorites of seafood gourmets, such as soles, flounders, plaice, halibuts and turbots.

When first born, the young flatfish swim upright and are shaped like normal fish. As they grow, they lean to one side and the eye on the underside migrates across the top of the head toward the other. Both eyes end up on one side; the left side in the flounder family Bothidae, the right side in the flounder family Pleuronectidae and in the sole family Soleidae. In some species, the eye migrates randomly to either side, causing confusion among biologists attempting to classify the many kinds of flatfishes. Their mouths, well equipped with teeth, remain in the normal position.

Curlfin turbot
Pleuronichthys decurrens

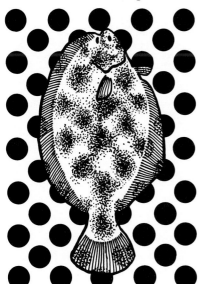

Flounders and other flatfish match whatever background they come to rest on, even a checkerboard.

Young flatfish look like normal fish but soon lean to one side and become bottom-dwellers.

The curious-looking result is an adult flatfish that occasionally swims sideways, but usually settles to a life on the bottom. Many species are masters of camouflage, blending in with whatever background color and pattern on which they come to rest, even matching a checkerboard in a laboratory experiment. Colored pigments within special cells in the skin spread out to darken the body, or shrink until it appears light, stimulated by what the flounder sees. In the Aquarium, flounders are displayed in a tank with two different backgrounds — white sand and dark gravel — to illustrate their remarkable adaptation.

Like other flatfishes, the ocellated flounder, *Ancylopsetta quadrocellata,* pictured swimming and at rest, has a white underside, which is normally hidden as it lies on the bottom.

The striking pattern of spots on its topside can be altered to blend in with its background.

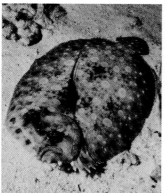

Peacock flounder
Bothus lunatus

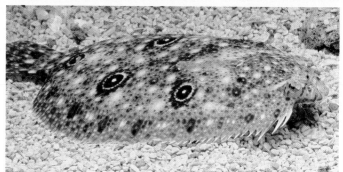

Lefteyed Flounders, Turbots

family Bothidae   order Pleuronectiformes

Turbots, *Scophthalmus maximus,* are lefteyed flatfishes of great reknown and commercial value, especially in Europe. They inhabit the shallows of the North Atlantic and Mediterranean, where adults grow to lengths of three feet. Each female may lay up to ten million eggs.

A small relative, the American sand flounder, *S. aquous,* has little value. It is so thin that light can be seen through it, hence the nickname "windowpane."

While this family of flatfishes is characterized by being lefteyed, over half of the California halibuts, *Paralichthys californicus,* have eyes on their right sides. Found off the coast of California, these large fish reach lengths of five feet and a record weight of more than 61 pounds. Commercial fishermen net them in trawls to meet the demand of the marketplace, competing with natural predators, which include electric rays, sea lions and whales, for the declining numbers of halibuts.

Other commercially valuable flatfishes called halibuts are in the flounder family Pleuronectidae.

The summer flounder, *Paralichthys dentatus,* is named for its habit of migrating toward shore as coastal waters warm. These three-foot-long flounders are extremely abundant in the Atlantic from Maine to South Carolina, to the delight of sport and commercial fishermen.

Few flounders are brightly colored. However, orange spots distinguish male Pacific sanddabs, *Citharichthys sordidus.* These are small but valuable flounders that are abundant on the California coast and popular on seafood menus. Atlantic ocellated flounders, *Ancylopsetta,* also bear a striking pattern of spots on their sides, but only those of the pretty peacock flounder, *Bothus lunatus,* are vivid blue. The latter ranges throughout the Caribbean.

Righteyed Flounders, Halibuts

family Pleuronectidae   order Pleuronectiformes

This family of righteyed flounders includes several species called soles, although none is the restauranteur's favorite, the true Dover sole of the family Soleidae. It also includes the king of the flatfishes, the mighty halibut.

Halibuts, *Hippoglossus,* feed voraciously on fish, including other flatfishes. They roam the deeper waters off both American coasts. The Atlantic species, *H. hippoglossus,* measures eight feet and the Pacific

Juvenile winter flounder
Pseudopleuronectes americanus

counterpart, *H. stenolepis,* reaches lengths of nearly nine feet. Known to weigh as much as 500 pounds, most catches yield halibut that average 25 pounds.

Included in this family is the most important flatfish in European fisheries, the plaice, *Pleuronectes platessa.* A three-foot-long species, it is well known in the shallows of the Mediterranean.

In the Atlantic, winter flounders, *Pseudopleuronectes americanus,* head into colder, shallow water with the onset of winter, taking the place of the summer flounders. There they often bite off the siphons of soft-shell clams sticking out of the sand, or feed on other bottom-dwelling creatures. Their range extends from Labrador to Georgia.

Soles

family Soleidae   order Pleuronectiformes

Soles are righteyed flatfishes. Most famous of the flatfishes and source of the delicious "filet of sole" is the true Dover sole, *Solea solea,* found only in European waters in the east Atlantic. Fishermen catch most at night when they leave hiding places in the sand to seek worms, brittle stars and other bottom-dwelling animals. Dover soles grow to lengths of 20 inches.

Hogchokers, *Trinectes maculatus,* are dwarves among soles, rarely exceeding eight inches. Their rough scales reportedly choked hogs that attempted to eat some found on the beach. Further recognized by their rounded noses, hogchokers live in shallow coastal waters, estuaries and occasionally freshwater rivers. They frequent the Atlantic and Gulf coasts of North America, where they are collected as a favorite exhibit animal.

Hogchoker
Trinectes maculatus

Triggerfishes, Filefishes

family Balistidae   order Tetraodontiformes

A triggerfish slowly winds its way through the corals, propelled by waving its upper and lower fins back and forth. At the first sign of danger, it darts into a crevice and raises the stout spine on its head, wedging itself in tightly. A second smaller spine locks the first one upright, and must be depressed, like a trigger, before the larger spine can be lowered. Even the most ardent predator or diver won't budge the triggerfish without breaking the corals, or "triggering" its release. The erect spines also make the fish appear larger, and present a sharp mouthful to would-be-predators.

Well suited to their shallow tropical reef habitats, odd-shaped triggerfishes fit into narrow openings and are covered with tough, leathery scales that protect them from sharp corals. Their large eyes move independently, ever-watchful for both danger and food. These are located well back from the mouth, safe from puncture by the long, sharp spines of a favorite prey, sea urchins. A hungry triggerfish will "blow" the urchin over with puffs of water to get at the unprotected underbelly, or pick it up by a spine and drop it upside down. Powerful jaws and eight strong teeth easily crush these and other hard-shelled sea creatures, such as clams and crabs. They even snip out the eyes of other fish.

Clown triggerfish
Balistoides niger

Solitary and often aggressive, many species fare best when displayed alone. Most belligerent of all may be the orange-striped triggerfish, *Balistapus undulatus,* equipped with several nasty curving spines on either side of its tail. These can inflict wounds when sideslapped against another fish.

The beautiful patterns and colors worn by these feisty fishes clearly signal their temperaments. The Atlantic queen triggerfish, *Balistes vetula,* has vivid blue cheek paint in addition to its regal oranges and greens. Most outlandish of all, the rare clown triggerfish, *Balistoides niger,* screams for attention with spots and stripes of white, orange and yellow splashed on a jet-black background. Little wonder this small, ten-inch fish from the Pacific is highly sought for aquariums. Black

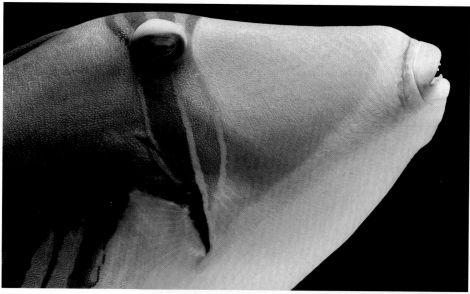

Picasso triggerfish
Rhinecanthus aculeatus

Sargassum triggerfish
Xanthichthys ringens

Queen triggerfish
Balistes vetula

durgons, *Melichthys niger,* sometimes occur in such
large numbers that the water is black with their bodies.
They thrive in the Coral Reef Exhibit where they have
plenty of room to swim even when they approach their
adult size of 20 inches.

The pink-tailed triggerfish, *Melichthys vidua,* is a
mild-mannered species that tolerates others nearby. It
includes large amounts of algae in its diet.

Several species of triggerfishes are caught for food,
despite occasional cases of poisonings.

Reef fishermen hauling triggerfishes out of the water
attest to the loud grunts they produce. Their vocal
abilities, plus the needle-like spines, inspire the
Hawaiian name for two common Pacific species in the
genus *Rhinecanthus: Humuhumu-nukunuku-a-pua'a,*
"the fish that sews and grunts like a pig."

A few triggerfishes have abandoned the security of
shallow reefs for life in the open sea. The young of one
such species, the sargassum triggerfish, *Xanthichthys
ringens,* relies on camouflage to blend into the floating
masses of sargassum drifting in the Atlantic. Adults
cruise surface waters, feeding on plankton.

The ocean triggerfish, *Canthidermis sufflamen,* also
feeds on plankton well offshore in the Atlantic. Largest
of the family, it grows to more than two feet.

Filefishes are docile relatives of the triggerfishes. They
share the family trait of a long, erectible spine on their
backs, although it does not lock. Like triggerfishes, they
also have a small spine on their undersides. When

both are raised to full height, the fish may appear too large to swallow, or may be too difficult to get down.

These timid fishes usually rely on camouflage and mimicry to fool predators. Some drift head down among blades of turtlegrass, swaying in currents. Filefish also change colors as they move over the reef feeding on gorgonians, algae, hydroids, sea anemones and stinging corals.

Largest of these retiring reef fishes is the three-foot-long scrawled filefish, *Aluterus scriptus,* found in tropical seas worldwide.

Planehead filefish
Monacanthus hispidus

Juvenile horned cowfish,
Lactoria cornuta (left) and
adult thornback boxfish,
Rhinesomas gibbosus (right).

Boxfishes, Cowfishes, Trunkfishes

family Ostraciidae   order Tetraodontiformes

Boxfishes or trunkfishes are odd-looking tropical reef fishes that slowly cruise the shallows, well protected by hard, colorful "shells." Only their mouths, eyes and rapidly sculling fins are exposed.

Those with horns over their eyes are known as cowfish, such as the scrawled cowfish, *Lactophrys quadricornis.* Other species are distinguished by the varying angles, ridges, spines and colors decorating their peculiar hard coverings.

When startled or alarmed, several trunkfishes, *Ostracion,* produce a toxin. Its lethal potency deters predators and quickly kills fish confined in the same exhibit.

Most boxfishes are small. Few attain the 20 inches of the blue-spotted boxfish, *Ostracion tuberculatus.*

Pacific islanders reportedly roast trunkfishes in their shells, like chestnuts.

Pufferfishes

family Tetraodontidae   order Tetraodontiformes

A slow-swimming pufferfish may seem an easy target to reef predators. When threatened, however, it suddenly gulps water and expands into a globe or balloon too large to swallow. Many also have tiny spines covering their skins.

Inflated pufferfish
Arothon sp.

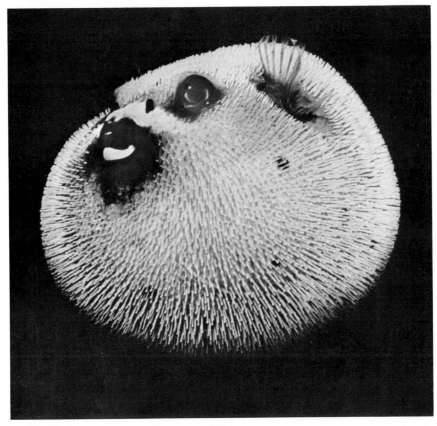

When pulled out of the water, pufferfishes also swallow air and, if thrown back, float helplessly, belly up, at the surface.

Pufferfishes are considered good eating, particularly in Japan, but because their organs contain a deadly tetrodotoxin, only specialty cooks may prepare "fugu." *Maki maki,* the Hawaiian name of the puffer *Arothron hispidus,* means "deadly death."

Pufferfishes bite through hermit crab shells, oysters, clams and snails with their strong dentition, divided into two upper and two lower teeth, hence *tetraodon,* meaning "four teeth."

Found worldwide in shallow tropical and temperate seas, pufferfishes live near reefs, seagrass beds and mangrove swamps. Some enter fresh water. River pufferfishes, *Tetraodon,* from Asia and Africa, are ideal and favored aquarium species because of their small sizes, docile natures and pretty colors. Equally popular are five-inch-long sharpnosed puffers, *Canthigaster,* which delight visitors with their comical movements and polka-dotted or striped costumes.

Striped puffer
Tetraodon immaculatus

Sharpnosed pufferfish
Canthigaster rostrata

River puffer
Tetraodon fluviatilis

Porcupinefishes, Burrfishes

family Diodontidae   order Tetraodontiformes

Porcupinefishes inflate like pufferfishes, but further discourage predators with conspicuous armor of dangerous, sharp spines. These are usually held flat until a disturbance causes the fish to gulp water or air. The resulting quill-covered sphere is as large as a beach ball in the case of the three-foot-long *Diodon hystrix.*

Burrfishes, *Chilomycterus,* bristle with short, rigid spines that are always held erect. Stories tell of Indo-Pacific natives wearing helmets of dried burrfish skin. Curio shops abound with dried, inflated, varnished versions of these unusual fishes.

These small fishes have pretty, brightly colored eyes and often befriend aquarists, accepting food from their hands, but their parrot-like beaks are potentially dangerous. *Diodon* means "two teeth," a characteristic that further distinguishes porcupinefishes and burrfishes from puffers. Both families are found in tropical and temperate coastal habitats worldwide.

Striped burrfish
Chilomycterus schoepfi

Inflated balloonfish
Diodon holocanthus

Amphibians

Amphibians — salamanders, frogs and toads — were the first vertebrates to successfully colonize land. Although most of them go through an aquatic phase before moving onto the land (amphibian means "double life"), a few are entirely terrestrial, while others remain aquatic throughout their lives.

Amphibians usually begin life as gilled larvae, hatched from soft eggs layed in water. After living for a while underwater, they undergo a change of form called metamorphosis. In amphibians, this transformation into the adult form usually involves the loss of gills, development of legs, loss or modification of the tail and development of sexual characteristics. These changes are not complete in some species, which become sexually mature but may retain their gills and other larval characteristics into adulthood in a condition called neoteny.

Most adult amphibians differ from fishes in that they have lungs, four limbs as opposed to fins, more advanced circulatory systems and, in most cases,

Green frog tadpole
Rana clamitans

scaleless skins. These differences enable them to survive away from water.

Adults are carnivorous, feeding on insects, worms, snails and other small animals. Frog tadpoles feed on algae and aquatic plants, while other amphibian larvae may eat small aquatic animals as well.

Once formed, amphibian skin does not enlarge so it must be shed periodically as the animal grows.

In their natural environments, amphibians are harmless, interesting animals. They spread no diseases, do not eat crops and do not inflict poisonous bites or stings, although some have poison glands in their skins for defense. Salamanders are secretive and rarely seen. Frogs and toads, which enliven spring evenings with their mating calls, often prey on insect pests. Some larger species have minor economic importance as food. Only a few of the estimated 3,000 amphibian species are displayed at the Aquarium.

Salamanders

Salamanders are elongate, tailed amphibians with legs. They are mostly secretive, land-dwelling animals that frequently hide beneath rocks, leaves, bark or within rotting logs where they can keep their skins moist. They feed on the worms and insects that live in these habitats. Most salamanders perform elaborate aquatic mating dances, often stirring the water vigorously as many individuals swim about.

Amphiumas
family Amphiumidae   order Caudata

Amphiumas are a small group of eel-like salamanders found only in the southern United States. Living at the edges of swamps, ditches and sloughs, these nocturnal animals forage at night for snails and crayfish. They have lungs, tiny legs and grow to lengths of 40 inches.

Lungless Salamanders
family Plethodontidae   order Caudata

The lungless salamanders are the largest group of salamanders with over 180 species. They take in oxygen through their moist skins and therefore must live in damp hiding places. They are primarily terrestrial. Some have no aquatic stage at all, laying small clusters of eggs under moist rocks or logs that hatch as fully developed adults.

Sirens
family Sirenidae   order Caudata

The eel-like sirens lack hind legs and have very short front legs. Like the amphiumas, they are a small group native to the southern United States, living as far north as central Illinois. They retain gills and some other larval features even as adults. Sirens spend their lives hiding in the mud or submerged vegetation of swamps and marshes.

Giant Salamanders
family Cryptobranchidae   order Caudata

These large, slimy creatures with soft, flattened bodies and wrinkles of loose skin inhabit rivers in the central United States, Japan and parts of China.

Giant salamanders hide beneath submerged rocks and overhangs during the day, feeding at night on fishes, frogs, worms and crayfish. They have powerful jaws and can deliver a strong bite. Their eggs are laid in long strands cemented to rocks or logs to keep them from being carried away by river currents.

The Japanese giant salamander, *Andrias japonicus,* is the largest living salamander, attaining lengths of 54 inches and weights of up to 24 pounds. The one American species, the hellbender, *Cryptobranchus alleganiensis,* is smaller, growing to only 18 inches.

In spite of their ugly appearance, both the Japanese giant salamander and the Chinese giant salamander, *Andrias davidianus,* are endangered since they are sought as delicacies and for medicinal purposes.

Mole Salamanders
family Ambystomatidae   order Caudata

As their common name indicates, mole salamanders frequently burrow, living in holes, loose dirt and in rotten logs. Members of this North American group are therefore rarely seen except during their spawning migrations, which usually occur in early spring. Spawning takes place in ponds following a mating "waltz" in which males and females circle each other. Mole salamanders can be identified by their costal grooves (vertical grooves along their sides.)

Most of these salamanders are from five to eight inches long, while a few, such as the eastern tiger salamander, *Ambystoma tigrinum,* grow to 12 inches.

Tiger salamander
Ambystoma tigrinum

In at least one species, the spotted salamander,
Ambystoma maculatam, there appears to be a symbiotic
relationship between a green alga, *Oophila
amblystomatis,* and the salamander egg. Eggs
containing the alga have a better survival rate and grow
more rapidly than those without it.

In some areas, especially northern Mexico and the
Rocky Mountains, members of this family remain as
gilled larvae. They become sexually mature, but do not
develop any other adult characteristics. This is
apparently due to environmental conditions, such
as iodine deficiency or low temperatures. The most
well known of these neotenous salamanders is the
axolotl, *Ambystoma* sp. Found naturally only in
Lake Xochimilco in Mexico, this species has been
much studied.

Six species of *Ambystoma* are native to Illinois. A few, such as the tiger salamander or the spotted salamander, are occasionally displayed at the Aquarium in terrarium exhibits in Tributaries. Visitors are fortunate if they catch a glimpse of one as it leaves its burrow to search for a meal of crickets or earthworms.

Newts

family Salamandridae   order Caudata

Also known as the true salamanders, this widespread group is found in Europe, China, Japan, northern Africa and the United States. Newts generally undergo a complete metamorphosis, and the adults have lungs. The costal grooves are less developed than in the lungless salamanders. This family contains both aquatic and terrestrial members. Some aquatic species will live on land if their ponds dry up. Others, like the European newts, *Triturus,* become aquatic only during the breeding season. American newts, of the genus *Notophthalmus,* have a more complex life cycle, developing as aquatic larvae but then living on land as young adults. This "red eft stage" lasts for two or three years, after which the bright red efts become a dull green and return to the water, living out their lives as aquatic adults.

Red-spotted newt
Notophthalmus viridescens

Firebelly newt
Taricha sp.

Land-dwelling newts usually have rough skins and round tails. Those that live in water have smooth skins, webbed toes and flattened tails that aid them in swimming. In many species, individuals change between these two body forms as they change habitats.

Some newts make mile-long migrations to and from their breeding sites, returning to the same sites for as many as 11 years.

Newts found along the west coast of the United States, *Taricha,* have a powerful toxin in their skins. This taricha-toxin is closely related to the tetrodotoxin in pufferfish.

Red-spotted newts, *Notophthalmus viridescens,* and other species are frequently displayed in Tributaries. Several species are common in the pet trade.

Mudpuppies
family Proteidae   order Caudata

Mudpuppies, *Necturus,* are also known as waterdogs. These large, slimy salamanders live in North American lakes, ponds and rivers. Although they develop legs, mudpuppies retain their gills as adults. They eat any animal food of suitable size and are often caught by bait fishermen.

The olm, *Proteus,* is the only other member of this family. It is a cave species found in underground lakes in the southeastern Alps. Like the mudpuppy, it is also neotenous.

Mudpuppy
Necturus maculosus

Frogs and Toads

The largest group of amphibians, these familiar animals are found throughout the world except for a few islands, deserts or permanently snow-covered areas.

Frogs are commonly thought to have smooth skins, longer legs and sleeker bodies than toads, but this is not always true. The 17 families in this group are distinguished by skeletal differences. Members of different families may look and act alike because they have adapted to similar habitats.

Frogs and toads are more advanced amphibians. They generally lead the typical amphibian lifestyle, developing as larvae or tadpoles in the water before changing into land-dwelling adults. There are many variations on this theme. Some frogs carry their eggs in their mouths, while others protect the eggs in specialized pouches on their backs. Tropical tree frogs often spend their entire lives in trees, hatching in small pools of water trapped in the cupped leaves of aerial plants. Some frogs have no larval stage, developing into adults while in the egg.

Since many species burrow or live on land, only a few are regularly displayed at the Aquarium. Those that may occasionally be in the collection include the Lake Titicaca frog, *Telmatobias.* An aquatic frog found only in the high Andean lake, its baggy skin helps it obtain oxygen from the water.

The brightly colored "poison-arrow" frogs, *Dendrobates,* may infrequently be displayed. Their toxic skin secretions protect them from predators, and are used by South American Indians to make poison arrows.

Tongueless Frogs

family Pipidae   order Salientia

These strange, aquatic frogs scavenge any food they can stuff into their large mouths. They have no tongues, relying instead on webbed feet to fan food to them.

The African clawed frog, *Xenopus laevis,* has small claws on its toes. It is well adapted to aquatic life with a streamlined body and small, upturned eyes to watch for predators from above. It even has a lateral line organ normally found only in fishes and tadpoles.

The clawed frog was once widely used in human pregnancy testing, but it has since been found that many other frog species are suitable for this purpose. Clawed frogs are still widely used in embryological studies. They do well in captivity, adapting to a wide range of conditions and eating anything offered. In

California, pet clawed frogs have been abandoned in local streams where their rapid reproduction and voracious habits have caused populations of many native animals to decline.

A brown, pancake-shaped frog called a toad, the Surinam toad, *Pipa pipa,* blends in with the muddy bottom of South American rivers. Instead of claws, they have a star-shaped cluster of filaments on their fingers,

Surinam toad
Pipa pipa

Aquatic frog
Xenopus laevis

which gives them a delicate sense of touch, useful for probing through silty water or mud.

The female carries the eggs in small, honey-combed depressions on her back. They emerge several months later as fully formed, miniature — but no less hungry — frogs.

Firebelly toad
Bombina orientalis

Firebelly Toads

family Discoglossidae   order Salientia

Bright orange or red bellies warn predators of the caustic toxin these toads produce. When threatened, they display their colors by putting their hands and legs over their backs and arching their heads upwards.

The family name refers to the disc-shaped tongue attached to the bottom of the mouth. Prey is captured by a quick lunge forward. Various species live in or near streams and ponds. Firebelly toads, *Bombina,* are frequently displayed in Tributaries.

Toads

family Bufonidae   order Salientia

Fat, warty bodies make the true toads easy to recognize. Slow animals, they rely on poison produced by glands in their skins for protection. They do not cause warts as is commonly believed, but their toxin creates a burning

Singing American toad,
Bufo americanus,
with throat inflated.

sensation in the mouths of predators. The young also
produce this substance, and predatory fish quickly learn
to avoid toad tadpoles. The secretion contains a digitalis-
like substance that was used in earlier times to treat
heart disorders.

Toads live on land in forests, fields and prairies.
Although they are rarely displayed because of these
habits, a few American toads, *Bufo americanus,* may be
seen among the plants of the stream habitat display.

Treefrogs

family Hylidae   order Salienta

These small, agile frogs are found throughout the world.
Most live in trees and bushes, clinging to leaves,
branches and stems with the aid of suction discs on
their toes.

Although frequently abundant, they are hard to find.
Many have bright green or mottled coloration to blend in
with their surroundings. Being so elusive, they are often
named for the sounds of their spring mating choruses;
cricket frogs, chorus frogs and spring peepers gather
around ditches, ponds and flooded fields and fill the
night with their music.

Only four of the eight Illinois treefrogs are confirmed
tree dwellers. Blanchard's cricket frog, *Acris crepitans,*
lives in wet areas, well adapted to the many treeless

Bird-voiced treefrog
Hyla avivoca

prairie sloughs that once covered the state. Green treefrogs, *Hyla cinerea,* spend summer days hiding on cattail stalks in southern Illinois marshes. Another southern resident, the bird-voiced treefrog, *Hyla avivoca,* calls from cypress swamps.

True Frogs

family Ranidae   order Salientia

The most familiar amphibians, the true frogs are found around the world in a wide variety of habitats. Streamlined bodies and long, powerful legs give them quickness and great leaping ability. Bulging eyes allow them to spot predators and prey in any direction. In spite of these abilities, they are an important link in many food chains, being sought after by birds, mammals and reptiles. The legs of larger species, such as the bullfrog, *Rana catesbeiana,* are considered delicacies by many people, and these species have some economic importance. Other types are valued for their usefulness in laboratory studies. Most notable of these is the common leopard frog, *Rana pipiens,* a spotted North American species that frequents meadows as well as streams and ponds.

Two native species are frequently displayed at the Aquarium. The green frog, *Rana clamitans,* lives around ponds and waterways across the eastern United States.

Although normally solitary, this dull greenish animal is sometimes found in colonies in suitable ponds. Green frogs can be located in the wild by their twangy, loose-banjo-string calls.

The second species, the bullfrog, is the largest native frog, growing to eight inches. Also called jug-o-rum, both names refer to the call of this portly animal, a low, bass "br wum," which sounds like a bull bellowing in the distance. These solitary animals stake out territories along almost any permanent body of water, waiting patiently for any animal small enough to eat.

In colonial times, it was believed that bullfrogs purified drinking water from springs, a belief still held about other frogs in certain parts of the world today.

Originally found east of the Rockies, the bullfrog has since been introduced throughout the west.

Green frog
Rana clamitans

Bullfrog
Rana catesbeiana

Reptiles

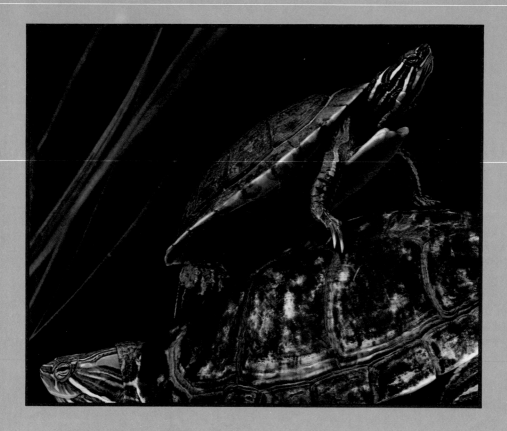

Although amphibians pioneered vertebrate life on land,
it was the reptiles that first developed the characteristics
necessary to make it a permanent home.

Two important adaptations, shelled eggs and tough
skins, enabled them to break their ties with water.
Leathery or hard shells protect the embryos from the
drying effects of wind and sun, and hold enough
nutrients to see them through their development to the
adult form. As adults, their tough, scaly skins protect
reptiles from desiccation and allow them to survive in
harsh, dry environments. With these adaptations,
reptiles colonized wide regions of the earth's surface.
Their feeding habits became more diverse, enabling
them to make better use of the new territories.
Carnivores, herbivores, omnivores and scavengers are
found in this group.

Although freed from aquatic life, many reptiles live in
or near watery habitats where they find both food and
safety. Many turtles spend their entire lives in the water,
only coming on land to lay their eggs. Totally aquatic,
sea snakes give birth at sea, and never leave the water.

Painted turtle, *Chrysemys
picta,* on a red-eared slider,
Pseudemys scripta

Protected by hard, bony shells, the turtles are the oldest living reptile group. These familiar, likeable animals are not viewed with the fear or distrust that many people feel towards serpentine reptiles. Turtles are long-lived, some reportedly reaching 180 years.

Turtles

Snapping Turtles

family Chelydridae   order Testudines

This North American family contains only two species, the common snapping turtle, *Chelydra serpentina,* and the alligator snapping turtle, *Macroclemys temmincki,* both ill-tempered and pugnacious. They are unattractive beasts with algae-covered shells, squat bodies and beady eyes. They have large, strong jaws and can deliver powerful bites. Although large specimens could crush a finger, the common belief that they can bite through broom handles is doubtful. Both species are used for food, although cleaning them can be a chore.

Alligator snapping turtle
Macroclemys temmincki

The common snapping turtle, *Chelydra serpentina,* is an ugly creature found in almost any permanent body of water east of the Rockies. They are aggressive on land but less so in the water, where they spend most of their time. Poor swimmers, snapping turtles walk along the bottom searching for food. At other times they lie in wait for prey. Their diet includes vegetation or almost any animal, dead or alive, including fish, birds, snakes or small mammals.

While many turtles sun themselves on banks or logs, snapping turtles bask in shallow water, often partly buried in mud where their dull, algae-covered shells provide further camouflage.

Although it can reach weights of up to 35 pounds in the wild, the snapping turtle is dwarfed by its larger cousin, the alligator snapping turtle. Weighing up to 219 pounds, these creatures inhabit large lakes and rivers in the southeastern United States, especially the Mississippi River system. The alligator snapping turtle can be distinguished from the common snapper by its larger head, the three sharp keels on its shell and the absence of saw-toothed ridges on its tail. Its mouth resembles a hawk's beak and is effective in catching and holding fish. It lures them by lying quietly, mouth agape, while wriggling a pink worm-like appendage on its tongue. Seeing something good to eat, the fish swims into the open mouth and is trapped as the jaws snap closed.

Common Freshwater Turtles

family Emydidae   order Testudines

Red-eared slider
Pseudemys scripta

This family includes the majority of turtles alive today. Most have low-domed, oval shells into which the limbs and head can be retracted. Except for a few land-dwellers, they are primarily aquatic, leaving the water only to bury their eggs in soft dirt near ponds or rivers. Basking in the sun on banks or floating logs is a favored pastime, since it helps to rid them of leeches and aids digestion by increasing their body temperatures. Wary and alert, even the most cautious attempts to approach them as they are sunning sends them sliding into the safety of the water.

The sliders and cooters, genus *Chrysemys,* are a large North and Central American group. The most abundant turtles where they are found, they can often be seen basking in groups. Ponds, lakes and rivers are preferred habitats, and individuals usually stay in a small home territory. They eat plants, molluscs, tadpoles and other aquatic animals.

Predatory mammals, such as skunks and raccoons, dig up turtle nests to eat the eggs. One can walk through nesting areas in early summer and see the broken shells. Young turtles are also eaten by snakes and other animals. In southern areas, alligators and alligator garfish prey on adults. Some are killed by people who

mistakenly believe that the turtles damage fish populations. Several members from this group can usually
be found in the Aquarium's pond habitat display.

The painted turtle, *Chrysemys picta,* is named for the
red or orange designs on its shell, a characteristic of
many members of this genus. These colors fade as the
animals grow older. Most also have red or yellow stripes
on the head. Millions of these turtles, and especially the

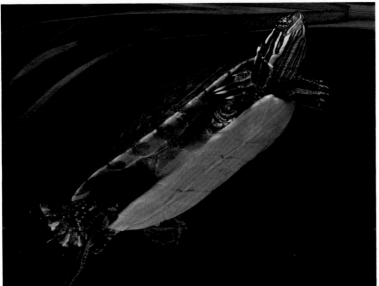

Painted turtle
Chrysemys picta

red-eared slider, *Pseudemys scripta,* have been collected
as hatchlings for the pet trade. Virtually all of these die
of malnutrition and improper care. This trade has
considerably lessened in recent years because of health
regulations aimed at controlling the intestinal bacteria,
Salmonella.

Closely related to the sliders, map turtles, *Graptemys,*
are shy lake and river dwellers. They are hard to capture
but are occasionally brought up in the nets of fishermen.
They feed on vegetable matter, molluscs, crayfish and
aquatic insects, the menu varying somewhat between
the species. As they grow older, plants make up more of
their diet.

The map turtle, *G. geographica,* is named for the light,
map-like tracings on its shell. It uses its broad, flat jaws
to crush the shells of molluscs. The false map turtle, *G.
pseudogeographica,* looks similar but has three prominent ridges along its back and is sometimes called hackle-
back. Both are commonly displayed at the Aquarium.

Named for the concentric grooves on its shell, the
diamondback terrapin, *Malaclemys,* is found in marine

or brackish coastal waters of eastern North America. Once hunted extensively as food, populations have been greatly reduced. An interesting example of changing values, this species was once abundant and commonly fed to slaves, but early in this century it commanded a high price as a delicacy.

Sea Turtles

family Cheloniidae   order Testudines

These giants roam temperate and tropical oceans around the world. Six species are generally recognized, although there is debate on the number of subspecies. They sometimes follow warm currents into more temperate regions, but do not permanently live there.

The streamlined shell and flat, flipper-like front legs are the most obvious adaptations these powerful swimmers have made to their environment. The smaller hind legs help them maneuver. They have lost the ability to retract their heads and limbs into their shells.

Sea turtles lay their eggs at traditional nesting sites on sandy beaches, either on mainland coasts or islands.

Ridley sea turtle, *Lepidochelys* sp., laying eggs at night on a Trinidad beach.

Studies have shown that animals return to nest on the beach where they hatched. This often entails a long migration to and from their feeding grounds. The exact distance they must travel is unknown, but estimates vary from a few hundred miles to two thousand miles for some populations of green turtle, *Chelonia mydas.*

These migrations represent great feats of navigation, and have stimulated much research to determine how they are able to find their way back to a precise site across many miles of open ocean. It is even more remarkable that nesting turtles usually arrive in large numbers over a short period of time. For example, Kemp's ridley sea turtles, *Lepidochelys kempii,* mate in a huge *arribada,* "the arrival." Archie Carr, a scientist who has intensively studied sea turtles, estimated that one *arribada* consisted of 40,000 turtles with 10,000 females nesting in one six-hour period on a short stretch of beach.

Once the turtles have gathered in the waters near the beach, the actual nesting begins. What triggers this is unknown. The females move onto the beach, usually at night, and attempt to crawl to areas well above high tide since the eggs would die if submerged. Once a suitable site is found, the female digs a nest, using her hind legs. The eggs are laid in this three-foot-deep hole, which is then filled in and smoothed over by the body. The strenuous, tiring process may take an hour or longer. Depending on the species and size of the female, 50 to 200 eggs are laid. These heavy animals move laboriously over the rough sand and must lift their bodies to keep their lungs from collapsing under the weight. When they finish, the females return to the sea to mate with males waiting offshore. Some species seem to nest at three-year intervals or, more rarely, every other year.

Sea turtles are threatened with extinction primarily because of their vulnerability at nesting time. The protein-rich eggs are sought by man and animals alike. It is not unusual for all the nests on a beach to be destroyed by egg collectors, or raccoons and other mammals. Many hatchlings die before they reach the sea, victims of predatory birds, crabs and mammals. Once they reach the water, sharks and other fish take their toll.

Tropical beaches are prime sites for condominiums, resorts and, in some cases, industrial development. Construction on a nesting area destroys its usefulness and dooms the entire population of turtles that instinctively return to that spot. When one realizes that virtually the entire population of Atlantic ridley turtles

Juvenile green sea turtle
Chelonia mydas

nests on a single beach on the coast of Mexico, it becomes apparent how fragile is their hold on survival.

Adult turtles have few natural predators besides man. In some areas, females are slaughtered for food as they come to nest. In addition, hawksbill turtles, *Eretmochelys imbricata,* are hunted for their shells from which jewelry or curios are made. Others sometimes drown in fishing nets.

Numerous organizations are working to preserve dwindling sea turtle populations. Their habits are being studied to find ways of aiding them. Programs to protect the eggs and hatchlings in order to increase their survival rate have been instituted. Commercial turtle farming operations have been generally unsuccessful. Sea turtles are protected by international trade agreements and all but the threatened loggerheads are endangered.

The sea turtles on display at the Aquarium arrive either from other aquariums or as juveniles illegally captured for the pet trade and confiscated by the government. The Aquarium serves as a repository for these animals, keeping only a few for display. The remainder are raised to a suitable size, then tagged and released in cooperation with conservation programs.

Green turtles, source of turtle soup, can weigh up to 650 pounds, although most average less then 400. In the wild, they feed largely on marine plants, and inhabit shallow lagoons where algae and turtlegrasses are abundant.

A smaller species, the hawksbill turtle is named for its hooked mouth. Most specimens weigh between 95 and

Hawksbill sea turtle, *Eretmochelys imbricata,* known for its distinctive overbite.

165 pounds. Hawksbills are found near reefs and lagoons, feeding on plants, sponges and sea urchins. Their shells are prized for tortoise-shell jewelry.

The loggerhead turtle, *Caretta caretta,* has a more varied diet. Conchs and shellfish are favored items, but fish, sponges, jellyfish and algae are also eaten. (The stinging cells of jellyfish cause swollen welts, often blinding the turtles that feed on them.) Loggerheads weighing 1,000 pounds have been reported in the past, but most weigh less than 300.

Smallest of the sea turtles are the ridley turtles. Most weigh only about 90 pounds, and are less than 30 inches long. There are two species: Kemp's ridley, *Lepidochelys kempii,* found in the Gulf of Mexico and along the Florida coast, and the olive ridley, *Lepidochelys olivacea,* from the northeast coast of South America and the Indo-Pacific. Why the ridleys should have such limited distribution, while other sea turtles are found around the world, is unknown. Another mystery surrounding these animals is their apparent absence in the Caribbean. The olive ridley nests on the west coast of Africa and is believed to make a 1,200-mile migration from feeding grounds near Brazil.

Leatherback Turtle

family Dermocheilida   order Testudines

The largest living turtle is the leatherback, *Dermochelys coriacea.* Averaging 700 pounds, some specimens may weigh up to 1,600 pounds. Similar in many respects to other sea turtles, this species is placed in a separate family because of its smaller, bony, shell plates that are covered with a thick, leathery skin. A powerful swimmer, the leatherback travels widely through the open ocean. Extremely rare, its habits are little known. Jellyfish are one of its main foods. Attempts to maintain leatherbacks in aquariums have been largely unsuccessful.

Soft-shelled Turtles

family Trionychidae   order Testudines

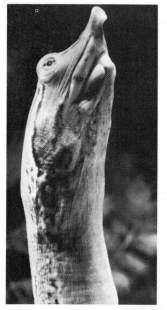

Native to Africa, Asia and North America, these active animals resemble rubbery, brown pancakes. The bony shell plates are reduced in size and covered by leathery skin. They bend their long necks sideways to withdraw their heads into their shells.

Aquatic animals, their snouts are drawn to a tubular point so they can breath, like snorkelers, without raising their heads above water. Favored prey such as crayfish, molluscs and aquatic insects are crushed in the soft-shells' small but powerful mouths. These turtles are considered to have delicious flesh.

The spiny soft-shelled turtle, *Trionyx spiniferus,* is a North American species inhabiting sandy-bottomed rivers as well as muddy sloughs and lakes. Large specimens grow to 16 inches in length. An Indian species, *Chitra indica,* grows to 31 inches in diameter.

The American species is commonly displayed. They can sometimes be seen prowling their exhibit searching for food. More often, they are content to lie buried in the

Spiny soft-shelled turtle
Trionyx spiniferus

sand with only their small heads exposed. Patient
visitors will eventually be rewarded with an eruption of
sand as the soft-shell, propelled by powerful, webbed
hind legs, heads to the surface for a breath of air.

Snake-necked Turtles

family Chelidae   order Testudines

The strange looking matamata, *Chelus fimbriatus,* has
a neck and head longer than its shell. The species name
refers to the loose fringes of skin that adorn its flat,
broad neck. Along with its triangular head and sculpted
shell, these fringes camouflage the turtle in the South
American rivers where it lives. Thus hidden, it lies in
wait for a fish to swim by. Small fish are lured closer to
the disguised turtle by the fringes of skin flapping in the
current. When one approaches, the large mouth
suddenly opens and the turtle quickly snaps up its prey.

Like the soft-shelled turtles, the matamata has a tubed
snout through which it breathes. The eyes of the
matamata are backed by a reflective pigment that gives
them a mysterious, prismatic blankness.

Adults grow to 16 inches in length. Members of this
family are also found in Australia and New Guinea.

Matamata turtle
Chelus fimbriatus

Alligators and Crocodiles

family Crocodylidae   order Sauria

These large, aggressive predators live in tropical areas
throughout the world. They are carnivores, feeding on
mammals, birds, fishes, reptiles and other animals of
suitable size. They generally stay near ponds, lakes or

quiet rivers, resting in shallow water with only eyes and nostrils exposed, or basking on nearby banks. Some species inhabit salt water.

Alligators and crocodiles are hunted for their meat and hides. Like other large predators that come into contact with man, they are also killed because of the threat they pose to life and livelihood.

Hunting pressure has threatened or endangered many species, and this group is now protected by law in the United States and other countries. The American alligator, *Alligator mississipiensis,* has made a comeback since being protected. They are now so numerous that a limited harvest of alligators is permitted in some areas.

Crocodilians require considerable exhibit space and are not usually displayed at the Aquarium. They can be seen at Chicago area zoos.

Snakes

A few aquatic species of these long, legless animals, familiar to many, are occasionally displayed.

Wart Snakes
family Acrochordidae   order Squamata

Oriental water snakes live along coastal areas of India, Ceylon and throughout the East Indies. Almost helpless on land, these sluggish animals spend their lives in water. The female carries the eggs inside her body until they hatch. This live-bearing ability allows her to give birth in the water without going ashore.

The Java wart snake, *Acrochordus javanicus,* lives in freshwater lagoons and rivers. It is also called the elephant trunk snake in reference to its stocky body. The rough, granular skin has been used for women's shoes and handbags, a practice strongly discouraged in the interests of conservation.

Colubrid Snakes
family Colubridae   order Squamata

This harmless family of snakes contains the vast majority of living serpents, and includes the American water snakes, *Nerodia.* They are semi-aquatic, living along the edges of a variety of watery habitats. On land, they search for frogs and salamanders, or bask on log jams at the water's edge. When danger threatens, they slip into the safety of the water. Graceful swimmers and divers, they also feed on fish and crayfish. Long teeth help to hold their slippery prey.

Young specimens of some species are brightly patterned, but as they grow older these colors generally fade to a dull green or black. Many are stout-bodied and are therefore difficult to tell apart from the cottonmouth, *Agkistrodon piscivorus,* of the family Crotalidae, a venomous species found in the southeastern United States. Water snakes will defend themselves if cornered, but prefer to swim quietly away to safety. The northern water snake, *Nerodia sipedon,* is common in Illinois and may occasionally be displayed.

Florida water snake
Nerodia fasciata

Yellow-bellied sea snake
Pelamis platurus

Sea Snakes

family Hydrophiidae   order Squamata

Most aquatic of all the reptiles, these live-bearing relatives of the cobras live their entire lives in the sea. Some 50 species live in the tropical Pacific and Indian Oceans. All possess a deadly venom, but many species do not bite readily and may not inject the venom even if they do bite.

Sea snakes shed their skins more often than other snakes. By sloughing off their old skins every two or three weeks, they remove irritating, external parasites.

The yellow-bellied sea snake, *Pelamis platurus,* is a wide-ranging species of the open seas. It floats amidst debris that accumulates in drift lines. Small fishes seek refuge beneath such cover and assure these pretty black and yellow snakes of an abundant supply of food.

Sea snakes, like all aquatic reptiles, must return to the surface periodically to breathe air.

Aquatic Birds

Many kinds of birds live near or on water, their bills variously adapted to feeding on myriad aquatic plants and animals. Oily feathers keep them dry, while webbed feet propel them over and through the water.

Penguins

family Spheniscidae   order Sphenisciformes

Avian champions of the aquatic realm, penguins cannot fly in air, but are superbly adapted to life at sea. Tightly layered feathers overlay their streamlined bodies. Thick coats of insulating fat keep them warm in chilly ocean currents. Their famous black and white tuxedos make them hard to see in water. When seen from above, their dark backs blend into the water; from below, white bellies are hard to see against the sunlit surface waters. Only the head patterns vary markedly between species, allowing penguins to recognize their own kind, even while swimming.

Peruvian penguins
Spheniscus humboldti

Penguins spend much time at sea. They "fly" through the water by flapping their flipper-like wings, moving fast enough to catch fish. When submerged, their feet act as rudders. On land, where they come to nest and molt, they can only walk and hop awkwardly, and resort to sliding on their bellies if they inhabit regions of ice and snow.

Only a few of the 17 or 18 species of penguins live in ice and snow, and surprisingly, all penguins live south of the equator. There are none at the north pole.

Each kind is adapted to its particular area. The larger birds, with the thickest layers of blubber and smaller wings that reduce heat loss, live farthest south, in the frigid Antarctic. Smaller penguins frequent the cold ocean currents flowing past the warm coasts of Africa, Australia and South America as far north as the Galapagos Islands, which lie on the equator.

In 1934, the small Galapagos species were the first penguins exhibited at the Aquarium. More recently, Peruvian penguins, *Spheniscus humboldti,* have been on view. They live in a display that simulates their native, rocky-coast habitat.

Year-round, these sociable birds leave the cold Humboldt current to nest in small groups on the warm Peruvian shoreline. Huge deposits of sea bird droppings once provided a soft material for nesting burrows. However, guano collectors have hauled much of it away as a source of fertilizer, and have nearly destroyed these breeding grounds.

Local fishermen further threaten wild populations by harvesting penguin eggs and killing adults for their oil and skin, or selling them as pets. (Natives call them *pajaro nino* or "child-bird.") Animals also prey on penguins on land. In the sea, sharks, leopard seals, oil pollution and overfishing of their natural food take a severe toll. The number remaining in the wild is unknown, and Peruvian penguins are now protected by international treaty.

In 1982, the Aquarium's youngest pair of penguins laid two eggs that were successfully incubated at the Lincoln Park Zoo bird house.

Penguins have lived for over 20 years in aquariums and zoos. At the Aquarium they swim and play in cold fresh water for health reasons. A shower every two hours keeps them clean. Salt, mineral and vitamin supplements are added to their twice-daily servings of smelt. Penguins are very susceptible to certain diseases, such as avian malaria and *Aspergillosis,* a lung infection.

Two-month-old J. B., one of two Peruvian penguins hatched in 1982.

Marine Mammals

Harbor seal
Phoca vitulina

Once land animals, marine mammals long ago became adapted to life in water. Most developed the following features: streamlined shape; layer of fat for warmth and buoyancy; and flippers, fins and tails instead of arms and legs. In addition, whales, dolphins and porpoises lost most of their hair, while seals, sea lions and others retained theirs.

Yet mammals that live in the world's oceans and rivers still share a few traits with their land-based relatives. They must return to the surface to breathe air. Mothers care for and nurse their young, which are born alive.

Whales and Dolphins

Whales include among their ranks the largest animal alive, the 100-foot-long blue whale.

Dolphins are spritely marine acrobats that dance through the waves of all seas. A few species migrated into freshwater rivers to escape competition. Their less-active lifestyle is well adapted to warm, shallow, muddy river and lake habitats. They swim slowly to avoid sunken logs and often rest on the bottom for hours.

Chico, an Amazon river dolphin, *Inia geoffrensis,* captivated visitors and staff alike with his delightful antics.

Only these gentler species, such as the Amazon River dolphin, *Inia geoffrensis,* have been suitable for display in the Aquarium. One of these, a quiet, docile dolphin named Chico, lived at the Aquarium from 1965 to 1982. He was one of the longest-lived of his kind in an aquarium and was at least 18 years old when he died.

Seals

Walruses, sea lions and true seals are known as pinnipeds, "the fin-footed ones," because of their large flippers. Unlike the whales, these furry sea creatures live both on land, where they mate, sleep and give birth, and in the sea.

Harbor Seals

family Phocidae   order Pinnipedia

As tides ebb along rugged, rocky, cold-ocean coastlines, harbor seals haul out to sun and sleep on the shore until high tides entice them back into the sea. On land they move awkwardly by crawling or dragging their heavy, blubbery bodies. Their hips cannot rotate forward like those of their more agile sea lion relatives, which regularly star in animal shows.

In the water, however, harbor seals are transformed into swift, graceful swimmers. Propelled by their strong back flippers, they hug their front legs close to their streamlined sides. Inhabitants of cold and temperate seas worldwide, they rely on thick blubber and heavily veined tough skin for warmth.

Efficient marine predators, harbor seals can dive as deep as 270 feet in pursuit of fish, squid, octopus and shrimps, or to pick shellfish from the sea floor. Their stout teeth grasp slippery prey, which they swallow whole, or crush heavy shells. The seals appetite for commercially valuable fish, such as salmon, once prompted bounties and hunting by fishermen to reduce competition. Brought close to extinction, numbers further dwindled due to habitat loss, overfishing of their natural prey and pollution. In northernmost regions, harbor seals have been hunted for their skins, for sport and for animal food. In Japan, oil is extracted from the blubber. The meat is used for pet food and waste for fertilizer.

Harbor seals are protected under the United States Marine Mammal Protection Act reauthorized by Congress in 1981. Protection was first extended in 1972, just a few days after the Aquarium received two year-ling pups.

The gray and white spotted female lived off Vancouver Island in the North Pacific with other *Phoca vitulina richardi.* These harbor seals range as far south as Baja, California. The brown and white male, *Phoca vitulina concolor,* came from the Atlantic off the coast of Nova Scotia.

This portrait illustrates a family characteristic: true seals (Phocidae) lack external ears.

Bibliography

Information is organized, for the most part, according to the following sources:

American Fisheries Society. 1980. *A list of the common and scientific names of fishes from the U.S. and Canada.* 4th ed. Bethesda, Maryland.

Barnes, R. D. 1980. *Invertebrate zoology.* Philadelphia: W. B. Sanders, Co.

Bold, H. C. 1978. *Introduction to the algae.* Englewood Cliffs, New Jersey: Prentice-Hall, Inc.

Grzimek, B. *Grzimek's animal life encyclopedia,* volume 5, *amphibians;* volume 6, *reptiles.* New York: Van Nostrand Reinhold Company.

Nelson, J. S. 1976. *Fishes of the world.* New York: John Wiley & Sons, Inc.

Ridgway, S. H. and Harrison, R. J., eds. 1981. *Handbook of marine mammals,* volume 2, *seals.* New York: Academic Press, Inc.

A detailed bibliography is available upon request.

Behind the Scenes

The non-public areas contain offices, labs and work
space for over 70 staff members and the many
volunteers required to maintain a large public aquarium.

Building Details

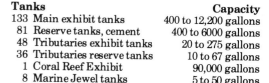

Tanks		Capacity
133	Main exhibit tanks	400 to 12,200 gallons
81	Reserve tanks, cement	400 to 6000 gallons
48	Tributaries exhibit tanks	20 to 275 gallons
36	Tributaries reserve tanks	10 to 67 gallons
1	Coral Reef Exhibit	90,000 gallons
8	Marine Jewel tanks	5 to 50 gallons
13	Sea Anemone Exhibit tanks	5 to 800 gallons

Building completed: 1929

Official opening: May 30, 1930

Original cost: $3.25 million

Replacement cost: $30 million

Shape: 300 feet in diameter, octagonal
100 feet high
30 foot terrace

Area of ground floor: 75,000 square feet

Area of mezzanine: 60,000 square feet

Area of basement: Over 90,000 square feet

Architects: Graham, Anderson, Probst and White

Exhibits: Over 200 exhibit tanks display more
than 5,000 fishes, invertebrates,
reptiles, amphibians, mammals and birds.

Average annual attendance: Over 1 million

Publications: *Guide to the John G. Shedd Aquarium,*
36pp., 1980

Aquatic Life in the John G. Shedd Aquarium,
272pp., 1983

Members' newsletters — *WaterShedd, Aquaticus,*
Educational materials.

Life Support

Aquatic life needs a constant supply of air and clean water at the right temperature. The Aquarium's three levels contain the enormous life support system necessary to keep the animals healthy.

From reservoirs holding over two million gallons, fresh and salt water is pumped through 75 miles of pipe to tanks near the roof, flowing by gravity to the fish tanks on the main floor and returning through filters to reservoirs in the basement. The total capacity of all the exhibit tanks is about 300,000 gallons.

Fresh water, filling half the exhibits, has always been pumped directly from Lake Michigan. The Aquarium makes its own salt water by mixing the proper chemicals with fresh water.

Spacious work areas behind each gallery contain reserve tanks for holding new and extra specimens.

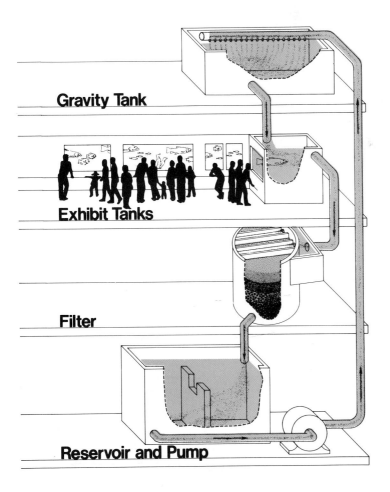

Gravity Tank

Exhibit Tanks

Filter

Reservoir and Pump

Care and Feeding

A wide variety of food must be cut, chopped, minced or ground to a size suitable for each animal. Over 31,000 pounds of frozen shrimp, krill, herring, squid, smelt, horse heart, spinach, other fresh seafood and prepared fish food are fed yearly. Vitamins and dietary supplements are added to the food.

Large fish in all of the galleries are fed twice a week, while smaller fish, penguins and mammals are fed up to three times a day. A diver hand-feeds the fish in the Coral Reef Exhibit several times daily.

The Aquarium has a well-equipped laboratory for monitoring the health of the aquatic animals and water quality. Treatments include adding precise amounts of chemicals to kill parasites without harming the fish. Antibiotics are another important health aid. Some health problems may require surgery or other services of the Aquarium's consulting veterinarian. The first corneal transplant on a fish was performed at the Aquarium.

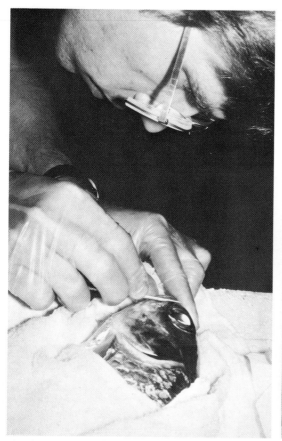

Collecting

Since 1930, Aquarium staff members have collected fishes all over the world, including Australia, Bahamas, Costa Rica, Dry Tortugas, Fiji, Hawaii, Mexico, Micronesia, Samoa, Venezuela and the Virgin Islands.

Until 1957, the railroad car *Nautilus* transported fish collected from the Atlantic, Pacific and Caribbean to the inland Aquarium located in the heart of the country's railroad lines. From 1960–1972, a higher speed, stainless steel *Nautilus* was used, while today fishes are transported by air in oxygen-filled plastic bags packed in styrofoam boxes. The Aquarium's research boat carries collecting crew members all over the Caribbean.

The freshwater exhibits have been stocked over the years with local fishes from collecting trips to nearby lakes and streams. The U.S. Fish and Wildlife Service and the conservation departments of neighboring states have been major contributors of native fishes, and were vital to the Aquarium's ability to remain open during World War II when travel was restricted.

Most tropical freshwater fishes are either purchased from commercial dealers or bred and raised at the Aquarium. Collecting expeditions have been conducted to freshwater rivers in Venezuela and Central America.

Other sources of fish have included exchanges with other aquariums, federal and state hatcheries and gifts and donations from private individuals, universities and research institutions.

Nautilus **1929-1957**

"A travelling miniature aquarium" built by the Pullman Company, the custom-designed *Nautilus* contained 35 portable tanks, three water systems, pumps, compressors and living quarters for the six-man collecting crew.

Displays

Habitat displays, the Coral Reef Exhibit, for example, represent the latest techniques in recreating community life, where many kinds of fishes are combined in realistic settings. These complex underwater scenes are created with artificial corals and sponges made out of plastic and fiberglass, using a procedure refined at the Aquarium.

Programs:

Membership

Membership in the Shedd Aquarium Society is available at a modest fee to encourage participation by the general public. The non-profit Society administers the Shedd family endowment, which is supplemented by income from admissions, membership contributions, donations, gift shop sales and Chicago Park District tax support.

Members receive many benefits in return for their support, including free admission, publications and visits behind the scenes during members' nights.

Education

In 1968, the first class for school children was offered by the Aquarium staff in an old office and in the public galleries. Late in 1975, the Helen Shedd Keith Aquatic Science Center opened on the transformed mezzanine. A library, classrooms, fresh- and saltwater laboratories, a conference room and offices were built on the lower level beneath the public galleries at a cost of $460,000. The Aquatic Science Center is named for John G. Shedd's daughter, whose generosity through the years helped create this learning facility.

Many special programs are available weekends and evenings for both children and adults. Classes are offered to visiting school groups free of charge during the school year. The library is open to the public and members by appointment.

Volunteers

Visitors can experience the underwater world through programs made possible in part by the Volunteer Program, started in 1975. Guided tours, evening lectures, films and summer classes are made available with their help. Each day, volunteers provide invaluable assistance behind the scenes in nearly every department.

Everyone enjoys Members' Night.

Handmade, artificial corals make up the Coral Reef Exhibit.

Volunteers help mend collecting nets.

Living animals enhance classroom and laboratory experiences.

Students seine in local rivers during marine biology course.

Index

Orange-tailed butterflyfish
Chaetodon xanthurus

A

John G. Shedd Aquarium
1200 South Lake Shore Drive
Chicago, Illinois   60605
(312) 939-2426

The Ocean by the Lake

Credits

Writer and Editor:
Nora L. Deans

Contributing Authors:
Roger L. Klocek: Invertebrates, Catfishes
Michael A. Rigsby: Amphibians, Reptiles, Plants

Consulting Editors:
William P. Braker, Becky Barefoot, Peg Kern,
Roger Klocek, David D. Lonsdale, Jim Robinett,
Linda Wilson.

Designer and Illustrator:
Sally Smith

Photographer and Photographic Research:
Patrice Ceisel

Production Assistants:
Jacquie Hemingway, Kay N. Schultz, Diane Smith

Color Separator:
Lehigh Electronic Color, Chicago

Printing and Binding:
Kingsport Press, Kingsport, Tennessee

Photographic prints:
Gamma Photo Lab, Chicago

Additional photographs: (page numbers in bold)

Shedd Aquarium Archives Building **6**, John G. Shedd **6**, Railroad car **8**, Octopus **43**, Horseshoe crab **45**, Blue crab **53**, Sturgeons **74**, Ocellated knifefish **78**, Brook trout **90**, Barred headstander **98**, Bigmouth buffalo **107**, Redtailed cat **116**, Tiger cat **116**, Ocean pout **121**, Treefish **140**, Tobaccofish **148**, Smallmouth bass **155**, Sharksucker mouth **161**, Emperor snapper **164**, Sheepshead teeth **168**, Black drum **169**, Freshwater drum **169**, Lemonpeel **181**, Giant gourami **209**, Snakehead **210**, Clown triggerfish **215**, Sargassum triggerfish **216**, Penguins **246**, Chico **249**, Harbor seal **250**, Collecting **255**, *Nautilus* **255**, Corals in Reef Exhibit **257**

Fred Bavendam Sea fan **36**, Sand dollar **56**, Herring **82**, Cod **120**, Hake **120**, Goosefish **123**, Lumpfish **146**, Jack **163**, Barracuda **190**

Steven Beal for Shedd Aquarium Aquarium facade **9**

William P. Braker Tucunare **183**, Electric catfish **113**

Townsend P. Dickinson/Photo Researchers Ridley turtle **238**

Douglas Faulkner Neon goby **201**, Moorish idol **204**

Lynn Funkhouser Diver **13**, Goatfish **15**, Lionfish **19**, Calcareous green algae **24**, Turtle grass **27**, Vase sponge **32**, Hydroid **33**, Fire Coral **33**, Reef **34**, Elkhorn coral **34**, Pillar coral **34**, Zoanthid **36**, Soft coral **36**, Fan worm **39**, Cuttlefish **44**, Basket star **55**, Crinoid **55**, Sea squirts **57**, Sawfish **67**, Green moray **85**, Vermillion grouper 1**48**, Bigeye **156**, Atlantic spadefish **174**, Queen angelfish **179**, Grey angelfish **180**, French angelfish **180**, Garibaldi **186**, Peacock flounder **212**

Al Giddings/Ocean Films Ltd. Tubeworm **22**, Shark **60**

Daniel W. Gotshall Horn shark **62**, Kelpfish **196**, Turbot **211**

Cleveland P. Grant Toad **231**

Roger Klocek Rocky shore **11**, Green anemone **37**, Squid **44**, Copepod **46**, Sea cucumber **56**, Lionfish **140**, Soapfish **150**, Member's Night **257**

John Kolman Skate embryo **69**

Kirk Kreutzig for Shedd Aquarium Aquarium **4**, Tusk fish **19**, Knifefish fry **78**, Mormyrid **81**, Gymnarchus knifefish **81**, Ribbon eel **85**, Milkfish **92**, Congo tetra **95**, Hatchetfish **97**, Redtail shark **104**, Chaca catfish **112**, Mailed catfish **117**, Batfish **124**, Halfbeak **125**, Four-eyed fish **128**, Walleye **158**, Sand tilefish **159**, Four-banded tigerfish **165**, Clown sweetlips **167**, Pinnatus batfish **174**, Brown chromis **187**, Tusk fish **191**, Mudskipper **201**, Paradisefish **207**, Cowfish **218**, Surinam toad **229**

John Lidington/Photo Researchers Jawfish **195**

Tom McHugh/Photo Researchers Hawksbill turtle **241**

Miami Seaquarium Mojarra **166**, Mullet **189**

New York Zoological Society Photo Metridium anemone **37**

Jim Parsons Grape algae **24**

H. Wes Pratt Sea lettuce **23**, Gunnel **198**

Hans Reinhard/Bruce Coleman Inc. Grayling **91**

Michael A. Rigsby Wetlands, Maine **11**, Seaweed **22**, Seaweed **25**, Mussels **42**, Brittle star **55**, Treefrog 2**32**

Charles Seaborn Coral, Philippines **11**, Balloonfish, inflated and deflated **16**, Kelp **25**, Mangroves **28**, Flatworm **38**, Chiton **40**, Nudibranch **42**, Skate **69**, French grunt **166**, Porkfish **167**, Blue angelfish **179**, Blue parrotfish **194**, Parrotfish in cocoon **194**, Wolf-eel **199**, Puffer, inflated **219**, Porcupinefish, inflated **221**

Bill Shaw Ribbontail ray **70**

Connie Shaw Bristle worm **39**

Jane Shaw Encrusting sponges **32**, Sea urchin **56**

Diane Smith for Shedd Aquarium Coral Reef Exhibit **13**

Steinhart Aquarium, San Francisco Striped bass **147**

Dr. D. P. Wilson/Eric and David Hosking Stickleback nest **138**